THE ABUNDANT LIFE
BIBLE
AMPLIFIER

PETER
& JUDE

ROBERT M. JOHNSTON

THE ABUNDANT LIFE
BIBLE
AMPLIFIER

PETER
& JUDE

**Living in
Dangerous Times**

GEORGE R. KNIGHT
General Editor

Pacific Press Publishing Association
Boise, Idaho
Oshawa, Ontario, Canada

Edited by B. Russell Holt
Designed by Tim Larson
Typeset in 11/14 Janson Text

Copyright © 1995 by
Pacific Press Publishing Association
Printed in the United States of America
All Rights Reserved

ISBN 0-8163-1247-8 (paper)
ISBN 0-8163-1248-6 (hard)

99 98 97 96 95 • 1 2 3 4 5

CONTENTS

To Madeline,
who graciously endured the writing of this book.

GENERAL PREFACE

The Abundant Life Bible Amplifier series is aimed at helping readers understand the Bible better. Rather than merely offering comments on or about the Bible, each volume seeks to enable people to study their Bibles with fuller understanding.

To accomplish that task, scholars who are also proven communicators have been selected to author each volume. The basic idea underlying this combination is that scholarship and the ability to communicate on a popular level are compatible skills.

While the Bible Amplifier is written with the needs and abilities of laypeople in mind, it will also prove helpful to pastors and teachers. Beyond individual readers, the series will be useful in church study groups and as guides to enrich participation in the weekly prayer meeting.

Rather than focusing on the details of each verse, the Bible Amplifier series seeks to give readers an understanding of the themes and patterns of each biblical book as a whole and how each passage fits into that context. As a result, the series does not seek to solve all the problems or answer all the questions that may be related to a given text. In the process of accomplishing the goal for the series, both inductive and explanatory methodologies are used.

Each volume in this series presents its author's understanding of the biblical book being studied. As such, it does not necessarily represent the "official" position of the Seventh-day Adventist Church.

It should be noted that the Bible Amplifier series utilizes the New International Version of the Bible as its basic text. *Every reader should read the "How to Use This Book" section to get the fullest benefit from the Bible Amplifier study volumes.*

Dr. Robert Johnston is professor of New Testament and Christian Origins and chairperson of the New Testament Department at the Seventh-day Adventist Theological Seminary at Andrews University. Before coming to Andrews, Dr. Johnston served as Bible teacher and departmental chair in Korea and the Philippines for twelve years. He holds a doctorate in biblical studies with a concentration in New Testament from Hartford Seminary and is co-author of *They Also Taught in Parables*.

George R. Knight
Berrien Springs, Michigan

AUTHOR'S PREFACE

The best way to learn is to teach, and the writing of this book has been such an experience for me.

Several times I have taught a course on 1 Peter at the Seventh-day Adventist Theological Seminary of Andrews University. Teaching this course has not only afforded me an opportunity to make a careful study of the letter, but it has also placed me in stimulating conversation with some bright and inquiring students, not least of whom has been Matthew Kent, who has now embarked on a doctoral dissertation devoted to the structure of 1 Peter. I only regret that I could not have the benefit of his mature research before writing this book! But I am grateful for what he has already taught me. Another student from whom I learned has been Madelyn Haldeman, now professor of New Testament at La Sierra University, Riverside, California. I directed her dissertation on 1 Peter—if *directed* is the right word for studying a very thought-provoking document.

But perhaps my most educational experience has been writing this book. The endeavor to make plain and readable the messages of Peter's two letters and the letter of Jude has helped to clarify my own understanding. For this experience I am grateful to God as well as to His servants at Pacific Press and to George Knight, the general editor of the Bible Amplifier series. I pray that the insights received through this study and writing will be as great a blessing to those who read as they have been to me as I wrote.

Finally, I want to declare my sincere appreciation to my two editors. Dr. Knight has proved to be the ideal series editor. It is difficult to imagine how he could have performed his task better. My commendation also goes to Russell Holt, who did what needed to be done without yielding to the editor's temptation of changing things merely for the sake of imposing his or her own personal style and ideas. I have to admit that most of his markings really did produce an improvement! But I take full responsibility for any errors the reader may discover.

To all these mentioned, I give my heartfelt thanks.

Robert M. Johnston
Berrien Springs, Michigan

How to Use This Book

The Abundant Life Amplifier series treats each major portion of each Bible book in five main sections.

The first section is called "Getting Into the Word." The purpose of this section is to encourage readers to study their own Bibles. For that reason, the text of the Bible has not been printed in the volumes in this series.

You will get the most out of your study if you work through the exercises in each of the "Getting Into the Word" sections. This will not only aid you in learning more about the Bible but will also increase your skill in using Bible tools and in asking (and answering) meaningful questions about the Bible.

It will be helpful if you write out the answers and keep them in a notebook or file folder for each biblical book. Writing out your thoughts will enhance your understanding. The benefit derived from such study, of course, will be proportionate to the amount of effort expended.

The "Getting Into the Word" sections assume that the reader has certain minimal tools available. Among these are a concordance and a Bible with maps and marginal cross-references. If you don't have a New International Version of the Bible, we recommend that you obtain one for use with this series, since all the Bible Amplifier authors are using the NIV as their basic text. For the same reason, your best choice of a concordance is the *NIV Exhaustive Concordance,* edited by E. W. Goodrick and J. R. Kohlenberger. Strong's *Exhaustive Concordance of the Bible* and Young's *Analytical Concordance to the Bible* are also useful. However, even if all you have is Cruden's *Concordance*, you will be able to do all of the "Getting Into the Word" exercises and most of the "Researching the Word" exercises.

The "Getting Into the Word" sections also assume that the reader has a Bible dictionary. The *Seventh-day Adventist Bible Dictionary* is quite helpful, but those interested in greater depth may want to acquire the four-volume *International Standard Bible Encyclopedia* (1974-1988 edition) or the six-volume *Anchor Bible Dictionary*.

The second section in the treatment of the biblical passages is called "Exploring the Word." The purpose of this section is to discuss the major themes in each biblical book. Thus the comments will typically deal with fairly large portions of Scripture (often an entire chapter) rather than providing a verse-by-verse treatment, such as is found in the *Seventh-day Adventist Bible Commentary*. In fact, many verses and perhaps whole passages in some biblical books may be treated minimally or passed over altogether.

Another thing that should be noted is that the purpose of the "Exploring the Word" sections is not to respond to all the problems or answer all the questions that might arise in each passage. Rather, as stated above, the "Exploring the Word" sections are to develop the Bible writers' major themes. In the process, the author of each volume will bring the best of modern scholarship into the discussion and thus enrich the reader's understanding of the biblical passage at hand. The "Exploring the Word" sections will also develop and provide insight into many of the issues first raised in the "Getting Into the Word" exercises.

The third section in the treatment of the biblical passage is "Applying the Word." This section is aimed at bringing the lessons of each passage into daily life. Once again, you may want to write out a response to these questions and keep them in your notebook or file folder on the biblical book being studied.

The fourth section, "Researching the Word," is for those students who want to delve more deeply into the Bible passage under study or into the history behind it. It is recognized that not everyone will have the research tools for this section. Those expecting to use the research sections should have an exhaustive Bible concordance, the *Seventh-day Adventist Bible Commentary*, a good Bible dictionary, and a Bible atlas. It will also be helpful to have several versions of the Bible.

The final component in each chapter of this book will be a list of recommendations for "Further Study of the Word." While most readers will not have all of these works, many of them may be available in local libraries. Others can be purchased through your local book dealer. It is assumed that many users of this series will already own the seven-volume *Seventh-day Adventist Bible Commentary* and the one-volume *Seventh-day Adventist Bible Dictionary*.

In closing, it should be noted that while a reader will learn much about the Bible from a *reading* of the books in the Bible Amplifier series, he or she will gain infinitely more by *studying* the Bible in connection with that reading.

The Letters of Peter and Jude

This volume will lead you into three ancient letters, called 1 and 2 Peter and Jude, sent to people who were trying to be faithful Christians in difficult circumstances. The times and the world in which they lived were, in fact, similar in many ways to those that we face or soon shall be facing. The Christian religion was misunderstood, and believers were confronted by considerable hostility, hostility that, in places, was already beginning to boil over into outright persecution. The people who received these letters were suffering.

To make matters worse, problems were arising within the church. False, but influential, teachers were leading many good people astray with their deceptions. The behavior of these schismatic groups was often scandalous, giving the church a bad name among unbelievers and seeming to confirm some of the worst rumors about Christians that were going around.

The emphasis in 1 Peter is on helping the readers deal with the first kind of problem—the hostility of their non-Christian neighbors. In 2 Peter and Jude, the emphasis moves to the second kind of problem—the danger within the church.

Our three letters belong to the group known as the General Epistles, which also include the letter of James and John's three letters. The General Epistles are so called because they are thought not to have been sent to a single individual or church but to many (although 2 and 3 John seem to be an exception). Peter's two letters are related by being ascribed to the same author, the most prominent of the twelve apostles of Jesus Christ, but they are quite different from each other. In content and concern, 2 Peter more closely resembles the short letter of Jude, which is the reason this volume includes the study of Jude.

Because these kinds of external and internal threats challenge sincere Christians in every age, but especially those living near the end of time, the counsels we find in the two letters of Peter and the letter of Jude are timeless and forever profitable. Being a real Christian is never easy, but these letters will tell you not only *what* you are to be, but *how* to live out your divine calling.

How do we find God's real message for us in the Bible? We know this is an important question because many have come to wrong conclusions from their study. They claim to base their teachings on the Bible, but, in fact, they have imported their own ideas into the Bible! If we are to be "a workman who does not need to be ashamed and who correctly handles the word of truth" (2 Timothy 2:15), we must listen humbly to the Scriptures, and we must follow correct principles of interpretation.

The Bible is an ancient book, and at the same time, it is God's message for us today. The New Testament letters that we are going to study were written to real churches and real people who believed and struggled two thousand years ago in the eastern part of the Roman Empire. You can sense that fact by looking at the specific names of the places and people that are mentioned. We are separated from them by great gaps in time, geography, language, culture, psychology, and general situation. These writings speak to us too, but we have to bridge those gaps. That is the business of interpretation.

Interpretation involves basically two tasks. We must first discover what the text *meant* when it was first written and sent. To that end, we employ every bit of knowledge and every tool we can get our hands on. Second, we must discover what the text *means* to us today, else we are mere historians. How do we translate what applied to ancient people to our own situation? What value for us is the instruction given to slaves? Why did the apostle seem to speak against women braiding their hair? What does that mean for us? This book undertakes to help you in both tasks—learning what the text meant to its original recipients and also what it means for us today.

The first task of informed study is hard work, and there are people who devote their professional lives to it. It is a work of the head. The second task may also involve the head, but it is much more a work of the heart, and it can be rightly accomplished only with the guidance of the Holy Spirit. In theory, a competent unbeliever could accomplish the first operation (which is mainly historical and literary), but not the second. The reader cannot hear the voice of God apart from faith. Thus faith and works go hand in hand. When it comes to interpreting the Bible, faith without the work of sound study is fanaticism, and study without faith is cold. But both study and faith are dead without the work of obeying what we learn as we read the Bible.

If you understand this, read on and prepare to be changed.

LIST OF WORKS CITED*

Angus, S. *The Environment of Early Christianity*. New York: Scribner's Sons, 1917.

Apuleius. *Metamorphoses [The Golden Ass]*. Trans. by J. Arthur Hanson. 2 vols. Loeb Classical Library. Cambridge, Mass.: Harvard University Press, 1989.

Aune, David E., ed. *Greco-Roman Literature and the New Testament: Selected Forms and Genres*. Atlanta, Ga.: Scholars Press, 1988.

Balch, David L. *Let Wives Be Submissive: The Domestic Code in 1 Peter*. Society of Biblical Literature Monograph Series. Chico, Calif.: Scholars Press, 1981.

Bauckham, Richard J. *Jude, 2 Peter*. Word Biblical Commentary, vol. 50. Waco, Tex.: Word Books, 1983.

Berkhof, L. *Systematic Theology*. Grand Rapids, Mich.: Eerdmans, 1953.

Bromiley, Geoffrey W., ed. *The International Standard Bible Encyclopedia*. 4 vols. Grand Rapids, Mich.: Eerdmans, 1979-1988.

Buttrick, George Arthur, ed. *The Interpreter's Dictionary of the Bible*. 4 vols. Nashville, Tenn.: Abingdon, 1962.

Carson, D. A., Douglas J. Moo, and Leon Morris. *An Introduction to the New Testament*. Grand Rapids, Mich.: Zondervan, 1993.

Charlesworth, James H., ed. *The Old Testament Pseudepigrapha*. 2 vols. Garden City, N.Y.: Doubleday, 1983.

Dalton, William Joseph. *Christ's Proclamation to the Spirits: A Study of 1 Peter 3:18–4:6*. 2nd rev. ed. Rome: Editrice Pontifico Istituto Biblico, 1989.

Danby, Herbert, trans. *The Mishnah*. Oxford University Press, 1933.

Daube, David. "Appended Note: Participle and Imperative in

---

*This list does not include classical works that utilize standard referencing systems across various editions.

1 Peter." In Edward Gordon Selwyn, *The First Epistle of St. Peter,* 2nd ed. Grand Rapids, Mich.: Baker, 1981.

Elliott, John H. *A Home for the Homeless: A Social-Scientific Criticism of 1 Peter, Its Situation and Strategy.* Minneapolis, Minn.: Fortress, 1990.

Epictetus. *The Discourses as Reported by Arrian, the Manual, and Fragments.* Trans. by W. A. Oldfather. 2 vols. Loeb Classical Library. Cambridge, Mass.: Harvard University Press, 1979.

Epstein, Isidore, ed. *The Babylonian Talmud.* 18 vols. London: Socino Press, 1948-1952.

Freedman, David Noel, ed. *The Anchor Bible Dictionary.* 6 vols. New York: Doubleday, 1992.

Goppelt, Leonhard. *Theology of the New Testament.* 2 vols. Grand Rapids, Mich.: Eerdmans, 1982.

Green, E. M. B. *2 Peter Reconsidered.* London: Tyndale, 1961.

Hamilton, Edith, and Huntington Cairns, eds. *The Collected Dialogues of Plato.* Bollingen Series 71. Princeton, N.J.: Princeton University Press, 1978.

Hammond, N. G. L., and H. H. Scollard. *The Oxford Classical Dictionary,* 2nd ed. Oxford: Oxford University Press, 1970.

Hillyer, Norman. *1 and 2 Peter, Jude.* New International Biblical Commentary. Peabody, Mass.: Hendrickson, 1992.

Horn, Siegfried H., et al. *Seventh-day Adventist Bible Dictionary.* Rev. ed., edited by Raymond H. Woolsey. Hagerstown, Md.: Review and Herald, 1979.

Iamblichus. *On the Pythagorean Life.* Trans. by Gillian Clark. Translated Texts for Historians. Liverpool: Liverpool University Press, 1989.

Josephus. *The Works of Josephus.* Translated by William Whiston. New updated edition. Peabody, Mass.: Hendrickson, 1987.

Keener, Craig S. *The InterVarsity Press Bible Background Commentary: New Testament.* Downers Grove, Ill.: InterVarsity Press, 1993.

Kelly, J. N. D. *A Commentary on the Epistles of Peter and Jude.* Reprint. Grand Rapids, Mich.: Baker, 1981.

Kersten, Katherine. "How the Feminine Establishment Hurts Women." *Christianity Today,* 20 June 1994, 20-25.

Kistemaker, Simon J. *Peter and Jude*. New Testament Commentary. Grand Rapids, Mich.: Baker, 1987.

Layton, Bentley. *The Gnostic Scriptures: A New Translation With Annotations and Introductions*. Garden City, N.Y.: Doubleday, 1987.

Lightfoot, J. B., trans. *The Apostolic Fathers*. Reprint ed. Grand Rapids, Mich.: Baker Book House, 1962.

Lyall, Francis. *Slaves, Citizens, Sons: Legal Metaphors in the Epistles*. Academie Books. Grand Rapids, Mich.: Zondervan, 1984.

McArthur, Harvey K., and Robert M. Johnston. *They Also Taught in Parables: Rabbinic Parables From the First Centuries of the Christian Era*. Grand Rapids, Mich.: Zondervan, 1990.

Malina, Bruce J. *The New Testament World: Insights From Cultural Anthropology*. Louisville, Ky.: John Knox Press, 1981.

Marshall, I. Howard. *1 Peter*. InterVarsity Press New Testament Commentary Series. Downers Grove, Ill.: InterVarsity Press, 1990.

Meade, David G. *Pseudonymity and Canon: An Investigation Into the Relationship of Authorship and Authority in Jewish and Earliest Christian Tradition*. Grand Rapids, Mich.: Eerdmans, 1987.

Merriam Webster's Collegiate Dictionary. 10th ed. Springfield, Mass.: Merriam-Webster, 1993.

Michaels, J. Ramsey. *1 Peter*. Word Biblical Commentary. Waco, Tex.: Word Books, 1988.

Minear, Paul S. *Images of the Church in the New Testament*. Philadelphia: Westminster, 1960.

Moore, George Foot. *Judaism in the First Centuries of the Christian Era: The Age of the Tannaim*. 3 vols. Cambridge, Mass.: Harvard University Press, 1927.

Moore, Michael S. *The Balaam Traditions: Their Character and Development*. Society of Biblical Literature Dissertation Series, 113. Atlanta: Scholars Press, 1990.

Neall, Ralph E. *How Long, O Lord?* Hagerstown, Md.: Review and Herald, 1988.

Nichol, Francis D., ed. *The Seventh-day Adventist Bible Commentary*. 7 vols. Hagerstown, Md.: Review and Herald, 1957.

Paulien, Jon. *What the Bible Says About the End-Time*. Hagerstown, Md.: Review and Herald, 1994.

Philostratus. *The Life of Apollonius of Tyana*. Trans. by F. C. Conybeare. 2 vols. Loeb Classical Library. London: Heinemann, 1912.

Pilch, John J., and Bruce J. Malina. *Biblical Social Values and Their Meanings: A Handbook*. Peabody, Mass.: Hendrickson, 1993.

Plutarch. *Moralia*. Trans. by Frank Cole Babbitt. 16 vols. Loeb Classical Library. London: Heinemann, 1927.

Pritchard, James B., ed., *Ancient Near Eastern Texts Relating to the Old Testament*. 3rd ed. with Supplement. Princeton, N.J.: Princeton University Press, 1969.

Reicke, Bo. *The Epistles of James, Peter, and Jude*. 2nd ed. The Anchor Bible. Garden City, N.Y.: Doubleday, 1985.

Rice, George E. *A Living Hope*. Boise, Idaho: Pacific Press, 1992.

Robert, Alexander, and James Donaldson, eds. *The Ante-Nicene Fathers*. 9 vols. Reprint ed. Grand Rapids, Mich.: Eerdmans, 1981.

Selwyn, Edward Gordon. *The First Epistle of St. Peter*. 2nd ed. Reprint. Grand Rapids, Mich.: Baker, 1983.

Seton, Bernard E. *Meet Pastor Peter: Studies in Peter's Second Epistle*. Hagerstown, Md.: Review and Herald, 1985.

Sidebottom, E. M. *James, Jude, 2 Peter*. New Century Bible Commentary. Grand Rapids, Mich.: Eerdmans, 1982.

Sparks, H. F. D., ed. *The Apocryphal Old Testament*. Oxford: Clarendon Press, 1984.

Stauffer, Ethelbert. *New Testament Theology*. New York: MacMillan, 1956.

Tacitus. *The Histories; The Annals*. Trans. by Clifford H. Moore and John Jackson. 4 vols. Loeb Classical Library. Cambridge, Mass.: Harvard University Press, 1931-1937.

Thompson, Alden. *Inspiration: Hard Questions, Honest Answers*. Hagerstown, Md.: Review and Herald, 1991.

Tidball, Derek. *The Social Context of the New Testament: A Sociological Analysis*. Academie Books. Grand Rapids, Mich.: Zondervan, 1984.

Vaughan, Curtis, and Thomas D. Lea. *1, 2 Peter, Jude*. Bible Study Commentary. Grand Rapids, Mich.: Zondervan, 1988.

Vermes, Geza. *The Dead Sea Scrolls in English*. 3rd ed. London: Penguin Books, 1987.

White, Ellen G. *Christ's Object Lessons*. Hagerstown, Md.: Review and

Herald, 1941.

_____. *The Desire of Ages*. Boise, Idaho: Pacific Press, 1940.

_____. *The Great Controversy Between Christ and Satan*. Boise, Idaho: Pacific Press, 1911.

_____. *Selected Messages*. 2 vols. Hagerstown, Md.: Review and Herald, 1958.

_____. *Testimonies for the Church*. 9 vols. Boise, Idaho: Pacific Press, 1948.

Wheeler, Gerald. *Is God a Committee?* Nashville, Tenn.: Southern Publishing Association, 1975.

Witherington, Ben. "Why Not Idol Meat?" *Bible Review* (June 1994): 38-43, 54.

PART ONE

1 Peter

Living
in a
Dangerous World

Introduction to
the First Letter of Peter

There is no substitute for reading the Bible for yourself. But there are different ways to do it, and you will get more out of your reading if you read with a purpose. In just a few minutes, you are going to begin reading through Peter's entire first letter. But first consider: How might you get a handle on what the letter *meant* when it was first written and read? And what might it *mean* today to you?

Eric B. Hare used to tell a story that greatly amused my children. It was about a boy who put a bean up his nose—and it sprouted! This gave me the term for an important principle of interpretation. I call it the don't-put-beans-up-your-nose principle. It means simply that a mother does not tell a child, "Don't put beans up your nose!" unless he has done it or appears to be about to do it. Otherwise, she is just giving him a dangerous idea he might otherwise not have had. Applied to biblical interpretation, the don't-put-beans-up-your-nose principle means that a writer always has a reason for writing what he writes, and that reason is that *his readers need it*. A letter such as 1 Peter is a mirror held up to the spiritual condition and practical situation of its recipients. With these things in mind, read 1 Peter now, trying the following suggestions.

1. **As you read through 1 Peter, keep asking yourself: Why did Peter need to say this? What does this tell me about the situation and conditions of his readers?**
2. **Make a list of the main themes and ideas of the letter, espe-**

cially those that seem to be repeated.
3. **Write down at least three texts that speak to your heart as meaningful insights for your own present condition and situation.**

Now that you have read through Peter's letter, let's talk about it.

Though it resembles some of Paul's letters, 1 Peter is distinct in many ways. It tells us a great deal about the nature and work of God (that word, *God*, is used thirty-nine times). It has more to say about suffering, both Christ's and ours, than any other part of the New Testament. Paradoxically, it contains the most concentrated theology and some of the most practical instruction to be found in the Bible.

Peter wrote his first letter from Rome ("Babylon," 5:13) with the aid of a literary assistant, Silas (5:12), who also helped Paul on occasion (see, for example, the greetings in the first verses of 1 and 2 Thess.). Obviously, Peter wrote this letter before his death, which, according to early Christian tradition, occurred during Nero's persecution in Rome, about A.D. 67. Since no general persecution of Christians took place outside of Rome before the end of the first century, certainly not where the addressees of Peter's letter lived (an area of what is now northern Turkey, 1:1), the difficulties these believers were facing must have been less severe than the afflictions that arose later. There were local persecutions, to be sure, but mostly these were problems of misunderstanding, suspicion, hostility, and harassment by unbelieving authorities, neighbors, former friends, employers, or spouses. In other words, for the most part, the believers to whom Peter wrote were experiencing the kinds of pressures that believers often face in our own day.

Purpose of 1 Peter

The people to whom Peter was writing had been converted not by Peter himself, but by other preachers (1:12). Most likely most of them had not been church members very long—perhaps ten years at the most. Most of them had come out of a dissolute pagan background (2:10; 4:3), and they felt the sting of rejection and resentment by their former associates, with whom the bond of wild partying was broken (4:4).

Many of the believers were wives of unbelieving spouses—rather less instruction is given to husbands than to wives (3:1-7). Many were slaves (2:18) whose new faith got them into trouble with their masters, who expected them to follow the religion of the head of the household and worship the family gods (Tidball, 79-86).

When believers were abused, cheated, or slandered, they had no one on earth to whom they could turn for redress. They could expect no sympathetic hearing from the civil authorities, who regarded them as peculiar at best, and even worse, as subversive. It seemed a hard load to bear. What was God doing? Was it worth it to be a Christian? The temptation to return to their former way of life was strong.

On the other hand, there were those who had heard something about Christian liberty, perhaps from Paul or his associates, and in their flawed understanding, they felt that Christ had freed them from the conventional rules of society (2:15-17). These were giving the church a bad reputation and reinforcing the impression that Christianity subverts "family values" by promoting insubordination of children, wives, slaves, employees, and subjects.

Although Peter himself had not raised up the churches to which he addressed this letter, he felt a responsibility for them. At the time, this region was one in which the church was growing most rapidly. He wanted to remind them why it is worth it to be a Christian—supremely worth it, even if it brings suffering in this life. He also wanted to instruct them about how to get along with each other in the church and how to relate to pagan society—when to conform and when not to conform.

By thus addressing the special problems of these young churches, Peter developed inspired answers to questions that have always faced believers who find themselves in the world but not of the world.

The Structure of 1 Peter

First Peter is a letter, not a book. When you write a letter, you don't usually sit down and make an outline of it before you write. You probably just pour out what is on your heart, and you may even repeat yourself sometimes. But in a general way, your thoughts flow in a certain direction, you deal with various topics, and there may be transitions between one topic and another.

That is pretty much what we find in 1 Peter. It follows the pattern of letters written in those times, beginning and ending with greetings (1:1, 2; 5:12-14). The main body of the letter can be outlined in various ways, but there are clear points at which the discussion takes a new turn, marked by words such as "therefore," or a direct address such as "dear friends," "slaves," "wives," "husbands," or "all of you," as well as "elders" and "young men."

Another way in which the letter can be divided is to notice Peter's pattern of giving counsel and then clinching it with a theological motivation based on a quotation from Scripture, an early Christian hymn, or the like. We find this pattern repeated at least eleven times. (1) After 1:13-15 comes a reference to Leviticus. (2) After 1:17 comes a hymn about Christ. (3) After 1:22, 23 comes a quotation from Isaiah. (4) After 2:1, 2 comes an allusion to Psalm 34. (5) After 2:4, 5 come three quotations—two from Isaiah and one from Psalm 118:22. (6) After 2:11, 12 comes a reference to the Sermon on the Mount (Matt. 5:16). (7) After 2:13-20 comes an appeal to Isaiah 53. (8) After 3:1-7 comes another reference to the Sermon on the Mount and another quotation from Psalm 34. (9) After 3:13-17 comes an allusion to the Genesis story as it was developed in the Enoch tradition during the time between the Testaments. (10) After 4:12-16 comes a reference to Ezekiel 9 and a quotation from Proverbs 11. (11) After 5:1-5 comes a quotation of Proverbs 3:34, a favorite verse in the early church.

The question is how to combine these smaller units into larger sections. For example, I. Howard Marshall wants to make 1:13 to 2:10 into a major division of the letter, stating the theological foundation of the Christian life, with 2:11 to 3:12 building in a practical way on that foundation by describing how Christians should behave in various relationships. But from another point of view, 1:13 to 2:10 can be seen as a continuation of 1:3-12, since both sections center around the general theme of salvation, first talking about its greatness and then about its results. It all just goes to show that the letter flows easily from one theme to the next, and how you outline it is a little bit arbitrary. But I suggest the following outline.

Major Themes of 1 Peter

It is easier to identify the major ideas and concerns in the letter than it is to outline it. That is because Peter comes back to some of these themes again and again.

1. *God* is not only in the background but in the foreground of everything. We can even say that 1 Peter implies the doctrine of the Trinity, for in it we find God the Father (1:3, 17), Jesus Christ His Son (1:3), and the Holy Spirit (1:2, 11, 12; 4:14).

2. *Jesus Christ* is central, as both Saviour and Example (1:2, 7, 13, 19; 2:21; 3:15, 18; 5:4).

3. *Salvation* in all its aspects, both as a future hope (1:13) and a present experience (1:10).

4. *The church* is God's flock and spiritual Israel, even when composed mostly of Gentiles who have come to the light (2:9, 10).

5. *Relationships* of believers to each other and to unbelievers is a major concern of the letter (2:11–3:9).

6. *Christian behavior* means that believers are to be holy and live so as to make a good impression on unbelievers, showing that the malicious rumors about Christians are false (2:11-17). Apparently this is

the real underlying concern in the letter: how Christians are to comport themselves in a hostile society.

7. *Suffering* was what Christ did for us, and we must expect to suffer for Him, following His example (2:21-23; 3:17, 18; 4:1, 2). Believers are opposed not only by human beings, but by the devil and his forces; however, ultimate victory is assured (5:8-10). The theme of suffering runs throughout the letter, but it is not so much the theme of the letter as the occasion of it. The real theme is how Christians should react to what they face.

8. *The Old Testament Scriptures* are inspired prophecies of Christ's work and its results (1:10-12; 2:6-8, 22, etc.). There are proportionally more quotations from the Old Testament in this letter than in any other book of the New Testament. The quotations are from the Greek translation of the Old Testament known as the Septuagint.

9. *The teachings of Christ* are also alluded to here and there, obviously as authoritative (for example, note the several references to the Sermon on the Mount in such passages as 3:9-17; 4:14).

10. *Church life*, its ordinances and responsibilities, is important (3:8, 9, 21; 5:1-6).

For Further Reading

1. For more details about such matters as authorship, date, structure, and an overview of the theological ideas of 1 Peter, consult a good book on New Testament introduction, such as D. A. Carson, D. J. Moo, and L. Morris, *An Introduction to the New Testament*, 421-431. For a more sophisticated discussion of the theological ideas, you may want to consult one of the books on New Testament theology that are arranged by biblical book, such as L. Goppelt, *Theology of the New Testament*, 2:161-278.

2. You may also consult the introductory chapters of recent commentaries. An abbreviated and simple one is that of I. H. Marshall, *1 Peter*. For more depth, see E. G. Selwyn, *The First Epistle of St. Peter*; J. N. D. Kelly, *A Commentary on the Epistles of Peter and Jude*; J. R. Michaels, *1 Peter*; S. J. Kistemaker, *Peter and Jude*; and N. Hillyer, *1 and 2 Peter, Jude*.

3. Of course, you should also check F. D. Nichol, ed., *Seventh-day Adventist Bible Commentary*, 7:547, 548; *Seventh-day Adventist Bible Dictionary*, 870, 871; and the article by Ralph P. Martin in G. W. Bromiley, ed., *International Standard Bible Encyclopedia*, 3:807-815.

CHAPTER ONE

Greetings to the Exiles

1 Peter 1:1, 2

Ancient Jewish letters began with a greeting that identified the sender (so the reader did not have to look at the end of the letter to find out who wrote it as we do today), then named the addressees, and finally bestowed a peace greeting. Most Christian letters followed a similar pattern, except that the peace greeting was expanded to include "grace," and some aspect of Christian doctrine was often attached to one of the three parts. That is what we find in the first two verses of 1 Peter. To the listing of the addressees, Peter attaches a theological expansion that introduces some important themes he will develop in the rest of the letter.

■ Getting Into the Word

1 Peter 1:1, 2

Read these two verses carefully, if possible comparing several translations. Then study them closely, and list all the important nouns. After that, read them again, and write down any descriptions of these nouns. After you have done these things, see what you can discover by referring to a concordance or other help. Answer the following questions in a notebook you keep for 1 Peter:

1. Using a concordance, list all the facts you can discover about the apostle Peter.
2. Consulting a good set of Bible maps, such as you will find at

the back of many Bibles, locate Pontus, Galatia, Cappadocia, Asia, and Bithynia. Note that the Romans administered Pontus and Bithynia as one province.

3. Do the words *strangers* and *scattered* have a special meaning? Would such words apply to natives of the regions mentioned? Note the use of the word *scattered* in John 7:35.
4. The Trinity of Father, Son, and Holy Spirit is found in these two verses. What relationship between Them and what functions are represented? In a few sentences, write down a description of any relationship between Them that is stated or implied; then list the functions of each as given in these verses.
5. Use the marginal references in your Bible and a concordance to discover the meaning and implications of the sprinkling of the blood of Jesus. See if you can find out the significance of sprinkling blood in both the Old and New Testaments. Summarize your findings in a paragraph or so.
6. Where else in the New Testament do you find "grace and peace" paired together as they are in verse 2? Is the order ever reversed to "peace and grace"? Why do you think this is so?

■ Exploring the Word

A Rock on a Mission

The sender of this letter identifies himself as Peter. That was his nickname, given to him by Jesus. His original name was Simeon, or Simon for short (Acts 15:14), son of Jonah (*Bar-Jona* in the Aramaic language; see John 1:42 and Matt. 16:17). When Jesus met him, He gave him the prophetic nickname *Kepha*, which means "rock" in Aramaic (John 1:42). That word was translated into Greek as *Petros*, from which we get the English name Peter.

Peter became the most prominent of Jesus' disciples and their usual spokesman. In all the lists of disciples, he is always mentioned first (Matt. 10:2; Mark 3:16; Luke 6:14; Acts 1:13). He was far from perfect, and we probably would not hire him to be a minister today, but the Lord patiently worked with him (John 21:15-19). He was the first to take the gospel to the Gentiles, almost against his will (Acts 10). That initiative brought him a lot of criticism from the brethren (Acts 11:1, 2). But later, when he and Paul divided up responsibilities, Paul accepted the task of preaching to the Gentiles, and Peter took responsibility for the mission to the Jews (Gal. 2:7). It may seem surprising, then, that this letter is directed to churches made up predominantly of Gentiles, as we shall see, but there is no reason to think that Paul's and Peter's division of labor involved exclusive franchises. Paul also preached to Jews throughout the book of Acts. In every town to which Paul traveled, he always began his preaching in the local synagogue. Similarly, Peter ministered to Gentiles even after he and Paul divided up their primary spheres of influence, as is clear in this letter.

Peter calls himself simply "an apostle of Jesus Christ." The word *apostle* comes from a Greek word meaning "to send out"—*apostellō*. An apostle is one who is sent out on a mission. The word *missionary* comes from a Latin word that means the same thing (*mitto*, "to send").

The word *apostle* has a rich background and history. The Jewish people were scattered abroad throughout the Roman Empire and even beyond, but they all looked to Jerusalem as their center. The Sanhedrin in the world headquarters at Jerusalem kept in touch with Jewish communities everywhere by sending out emissaries with messages and directives. Such a messenger was called a *sheliach* ("one who is sent"), which was the Hebrew equivalent of *apostle*. Paul was on such a mission to Damascus (Acts 9:2) when the Lord interrupted his journey and changed him from a Pharisaic apostle to a Christian apostle.

Jesus, as the Gospel of John frequently tells us (John 17:3, 8, 18), was sent by His Father into the world, and He similarly sent His disciples out (John 20:21). Thus His disciples became His apostles. Unlike the scribes and rabbis, who raised up disciples to themselves (Mishnah *Aboth* 1:1), Christ's apostles were to make people disciples of Jesus and to be conduits for His teachings (Matt. 28:18-20), not their own. They derived their authority from Him alone. All this was involved when Peter identified himself simply as "an apostle of Jesus Christ."

Aliens in Their Own Country

Besides introducing himself, Peter has a lot to say about the addressees. It is therefore the second part of the greeting that receives the theological expansion. For one thing, those to whom he is writing are "elect" or "chosen" (the NIV uses two words to try to express the thought, but in Greek there is only one word), and this choosing is "according to the foreknowledge of God the Father." These expressions could get us into the age-old controversy about predestination, but that would be missing the main point (although it *is* good to know, as the gospel song puts it, "Before time began you were part of His plan").

The Lord chose Israel because He loved them for the sake of their ancestors (Deut. 4:37; 7:7-10; compare Rom. 11:28, 29), and this choice involved both privilege and responsibility, because they were special (Amos 3:2), set apart from other peoples. "Knowing" means loving, and "not knowing" means rejecting (Matt. 7:23). Foreknowing means loving us before we loved Him. Because God loves us, He chooses and calls. God chose individuals such as Abraham (Gen. 18:19), but above all, He chose a people.

By applying the term *chosen* to his readers, Peter is saying that whether they are ethnically Jews or Gentiles, Christians are the New Israel, a point he is going to develop later. He mentions three factors involved in their becoming the chosen people. (1) The basis is the foreknowledge of God the Father. (2) The means is the sanctifying work of the Spirit. (*Sanctification* or *consecration* means "setting apart for a special use.") (3) The purpose is obedience and sprinkling of the blood of Jesus Christ. So all of the Trinity is involved.

God's foreknowledge points to His initiative in saving us. He called us because He first loved us, before we loved Him. He consecrated us by the Holy Spirit, through whom He called us. It is His call that sets us apart as special people. This privilege involves a responsibility: obedience. The NIV interprets the phrase as "obedience *to Jesus Christ*," though the Greek connects "Jesus Christ" with only the next phrase, "sprinkling by the blood of Jesus Christ." In this instance the obedience is specifically obedience to the gospel of Christ, meaning acceptance of it (Rom. 1:5) and of the teachings of Christ (Matt. 28:20). A word for that is *conversion*, which for first-generation Christians was inseparable from baptism. (In those days baptism was never taken lightly.) There is a parallel saying in 2 Thessalonians 2:13: "From the beginning God chose you to be saved through the sanctifying work of the Spirit and through belief in the truth." Verse 14 goes on to say, "He called you to this through our gospel."

The expression about sprinkling of the blood of Christ has a rich Old Testament background. When the people of Israel declared that they would obey the provisions of the covenant the Lord was making with them, Moses sprinkled blood on them, saying, "This is the blood of the covenant that the Lord has made with you in accordance with all these words" (Exod. 24:7, 8). Jesus was the Mediator of a new covenant sealed by His own sprinkled blood (Heb. 12:24). This is symbolized in the Lord's Supper (Mark 14:24). People were sealed into this new covenant by receiving baptism, and that was preceded by conversion. But it is Jesus' blood that brings us into a covenant relationship with the Lord. We renew this covenant every time we participate in the Lord's Supper.

This wonderful privilege of joining the new chosen people of God had a down side. Those chosen became a special people, but special people are not popular with other people who are not special!

Two words in verse 1 point to the fact that the addressees were not at home where they were living: *strangers* (to which the NIV adds "in the world" by way of interpretation, though these words are not in the Greek) and *scattered*.

This last word translates the Greek word *diaspora*, which is also used in English and sometimes translated Dispersion. The Diaspora is a term used for Jews living abroad, away from their homeland in Palestine. It is so used in John 7:35. The first Diaspora was the eastern one that occurred when the Jews were taken away into captivity and exile in Babylon. The second Diaspora carried Jews to the west— to Egypt, Asia Minor, Greece, Rome, and, ultimately, all over the world. As a result, wherever Paul went, he found Jewish communities and usually a synagogue.

But to the extent that Jews remained faithful to their religion and culture, they did not mix well with their non-Jewish neighbors. Because of their distinctive customs, diet, and religion, and because the more scrupulous Jews feared defilement through contact with the Gentiles, they were considered unsocial, if not antisocial. One Greek writer wrote:

> [The Jews] cannot share with the rest of mankind the pleasures of the table nor join in their libations or prayers or sacrifices; [they] are separated from ourselves by a greater gulf than divides us from Susa or Bactria or the more distant Indies (Philostratus, *Life of Apollonius*, 5.33).

The Jewish religion was also considered intolerant, for Jews believed their God was the only true God and that only He was to be worshiped. They denounced the making and worship of idols, kept the Sabbath, and ate no pork. Nobody else was like that. So the Jews of the Diaspora remained unassimilated strangers wherever they settled, no matter how many generations they lived there. They were generally tolerated, however, as foreigners, and the Jewish religion—unlike Christianity—was licensed by the Roman government.

But what were people to think about native-born people, even their own kith and kin, who deliberately made themselves alien? That is what people wondered about Christians. Gentile Christians were not Jews, but they were equally intolerant about the pagan gods and worship. Yet even the Jews seemed to disown them! When these people became Christians, they no longer associated with their former friends, neighbors, and relatives in the wild carousing that was often part of the idolatrous pagan cults and civic life (4:3, 4). They did not want to have "fun" with other people—they just wanted to evangelize them!

Besides, there were disturbing rumors about the Christians. They were accused of atheism, for they denied the pagan gods and had no idols. They were accused of incest, for they called each other brother and sister and talked about love all the time. They were accused of cannibalism, for in their religious services they talked about eating the flesh and drinking the blood of someone named Jesus. Many other ugly rumors were circulating, but the worst accusation was that Christians were subversive rebels against society.

Mostly what Christians faced was a matter of social discrimination, though sometimes vicious accusations would lead to individuals being arrested and dragged into court (4:15, 16). By the time 1 Peter was written, the level of hostility against Christians was beginning to rise. Soon a brutal persecution would erupt in Rome when Emperor Nero made Christians serve as scapegoats for the great fire that broke out there in A.D. 64. A Roman historian described them as "a class of men, loathed for their abominations, whom the crowd called Christians," and records: "First, then the confessed members of the sect were arrested; next, from the information extracted from them, a large number were convicted, not so much on account of arson as for hatred of the human race" (Tacitus, *Annals*, 15.44).

So it was that the addressees of this letter may have been natives of Pontus, Galatia, Cappadocia, Asia, and Bithynia, but they were no longer at home there. Even though they were mostly Gentiles (1:14, 18; 2:9, 10; 4:3), they were strangers even more than ethnic Jews, for there was nowhere in this world where they would not be strangers. That went with the territory of being the Diaspora of the New Israel (an image also used in James 1:1), the new chosen people. The time before Jesus returns is a time of exile (1:17), and it is no coincidence that Peter calls Rome "Babylon" (5:13), the place of the first Jewish exile. They had become sojourners and pilgrims, just passing through, just camping.

Grace and Peace

How paradoxical it must have sounded, under the circumstances just described, that Peter should pray for them to have peace! To be sure, peace was the traditional Jewish way of greeting (repeated at the end of the letter, 5:14). The Hebrew word was *shalom*, which meant much more than a mere absence of conflict. *Shalom* meant everything that makes for well-being, including good relationships with people and with God. Such peace could only be the gift of God to His people and would come only in the time of the Messiah.

For Christians, the Messiah had already come, although He must come again. He had established His kingdom of grace in the hearts of believers; the kingdom of glory was still future. So they preceded the word *peace* with the word *grace*. Most of Paul's letters begin that way (Rom. 1:7; 1 Cor. 1:3; 2 Cor. 1:2; Gal. 1:3; Eph. 1:2; Phil. 1:2; Col. 1:2; 1 Thess. 1:1; 2 Thess. 1:2; Titus 1:4; Philem. 3; 1 and 2 Timothy add *mercy* to the other two words). It is because the grace of God came through Jesus Christ (John 1:17) that believers could have peace—peace within, peace with God, and peace with each other—no matter what turmoil the world might pour over them. Grace is the basis of peace.

■ Applying the Word

1 Peter 1:1, 2

1. Are there people today who could be called apostles, even though they were not among the original Twelve? What makes a person an apostle? Is there some sense in which I can view myself as an apostle?
2. Peter indicates that Christians are chosen people. What does that mean in terms of God's plan for my life and for my sense of personal destiny?
3. List the ways in which Christians today find themselves in the same kind of situations as the Christians to whom Peter addressed this letter. Am I too much at home in the world? Is it wrong to be liked by unbelievers? Is it wrong to be disliked by them? Does it depend on the reason for the dislike? Explain your answer.
4. What does it mean to be sanctified or consecrated by the Holy Spirit? When did it happen to me? When was I sprinkled by the blood of Jesus Christ? What difference do these experiences make in my life?
5. Have I or my church ever been the subject of malicious rumors and reports? Were the reports at all justified? What is the best way to deal with such rumors and reports?

6. Why should I have peace in my heart? How is peace related to God's grace? What difference does grace make in my life, both in the way I feel about myself and in the way I feel about others?

■ Researching the Word

1. With a concordance, study the use of the words *elect* and *chosen*. Who were called "chosen" in the Old Testament? Who were called "chosen" or "elect" in the New Testament? Note when the words are applied in the singular and when they are applied to groups. Look up the topic "foreknowledge" in a Bible dictionary.

2. Make a similar study of the word *peace*. Note how it comes, who gives it, and to whom it is given. Did the people who received the peace of God ever experience trouble afterward?

3. Read the article on Peter in the *SDA Bible Dictionary* or some other Bible dictionary. What is the evidence for the claim that Peter was martyred in Rome? Does that support the Roman Catholic claim that Peter was the first pope? What are several things that would have to be proved in order to support such a claim?

4. With a concordance, find out who were called apostles in the New Testament. Was the term limited to the Twelve who had been with Jesus? Note that in Romans 16:7 the name Junias (masculine) should probably be Junia (feminine). The Greek could be either, but the masculine form Junias scarcely occurs at all in ancient literature, while the feminine form Junia is very common. Andronicus and Junia were probably a husband-and-wife team.

■ Further Study of the Word

1. For an insightful meditation on the career of Peter, as well as a helpful theological study of election and the issue of predestination, see G. E. Rice, *A Living Hope*, 7-24.

2. Perhaps the most detailed recent commentary, having also a

good discussion of whom the recipients of this letter were, is J. R. Michaels, *1 Peter*, 3-14 and xlv-lv.

3. A useful discussion of the social situation in which people of New Testament times lived is D. Tidball, *The Social Context of the New Testament: A Sociological Analysis*. Note especially pages 65 to 122. A sociological study centered on 1 Peter is that of J. H. Elliott, *A Home for the Homeless: A Social-Scientific Criticism of 1 Peter, Its Situation and Strategy*.

CHAPTER TWO

Salvation and Its Results

1 Peter 1:3–2:10

In the introductory greeting of the first two verses, Peter introduced several themes that he is now going to develop. The next section is largely an expansion of the three things he said about the Christians to whom this letter is addressed: their chosenness, sanctification, and obedience. We can divide this first part of the main body of the letter into two sections. In the first (1:3-12), Peter deals with the privilege of salvation; in the second (1:13–2:10), he examines the resulting obligations.

Peter begins with a traditional prayer of praise to God but shades off around verse 6 into a densely packed sermon. He discusses the implications of Christians' chosenness according to the foreknowledge of God (1:3-12), their sanctification by the Holy Spirit (vss. 13-17), and their obedience and sprinkling (vss. 18-25). He then returns to the theme of chosenness (2:4-10).

In the first of these subsections, the Trinity again appears, with verses 3 to 5 focusing on God the Father, 6 to 9 revolving around Jesus Christ, and 10 to 12 featuring the work of the Holy Spirit.

Because 1:3-12 is a theological statement of what the Lord has done for us, Peter phrases it exclusively in the indicative mode. Because the second section (1:13–2:10) deals with our responsibilities to God, Peter expresses it largely in imperatives, at least in 1:13 to 2:3.

Throughout this part, but especially in the second section, Peter piles up many rich metaphors. (A metaphor is a figure of speech in which we speak of one thing in terms of another that resembles it in some way, as, for example, when we say, "Your daughter is a jewel," or when Jesus referred to Herod as "that fox" in Luke 13:32.) A key metaphor toward the end of this part of Peter's letter (2:4-10) is that of the Stone and the stones. Another feature of Peter's (or Silas's) literary style that we begin to notice is the abundance of biblical quotations and allusions. (Remember, at that time, the only Bible was the Old Testament; the New Testament was still being written.) Peter apparently took many of these quotations from collections of proof texts that circulated widely among the early Christians.

■ Getting Into the Word

1 Peter 1:3-12

Read through 1 Peter from the beginning through 2:10 to get the overall flow. Then read closely this section, 1:3-12, noticing how it fits into the larger unit. As you read, keep asking yourself why Peter needed to say these things. If possible, compare another translation, and take note of significant differences from the NIV. Now give attention to the following points:

1. List all the terms and expressions Peter uses to refer to salvation. What different aspects of salvation do they bring out? Consider which ones are past, which are present, and which are future.
2. Using a concordance, look up all the places in the New Testament where the word *inheritance* is found, and note what it is that is inherited. After examining the word in the Bible, it will be helpful to compare your findings with an article about inheritance in a Bible dictionary.
3. Three times the first chapter of 1 Peter directly or indirectly contrasts the perishable with the imperishable (vss. 4, 18, 23). What specific things are being contrasted, and why are they contrasted?
4. What emotions and feelings are mentioned, and what reasons are given for having them?
5. According to this passage, what is the value of trials and suffering?
6. What aspect or aspects of salvation were foreseen by the

prophets? Which prophecies do you think Peter is referring to in 1:11?

7. Besides this chapter in 1 Peter, other places in the New Testament speak of being born again or being born of God (such as John 3:3-7 and 1 John 5:1). With the help of a concordance, list as many of these references as you can find.

■ Exploring the Word

Born Into a Living Hope

The people Peter was writing to were getting into trouble just because they were Christians, and some of them must have been wondering if it was worth it. Peter's answer is to remind them of how great a thing salvation in Jesus Christ is—so great that it is worth *any* trouble!

This section begins with a doxology praising God for what He has done for us. It was not uncommon even for pagan letters at the time to include such thanksgiving, but 1 Peter 1:3 follows a pattern exactly like that which Paul uses in 2 Corinthians 1:3 and Ephesians 1:3, addressing praise "to the God and Father of our Lord Jesus Christ." The fact that the phrase was customary did not make it any less sincere.

Note that the formula calls Jesus Christ "Lord." This was the basic creed of New Testament Christians (1 Cor. 12:3), significant because their Old Testament Scriptures applied that title to God (compare 1 Pet. 3:15; but in 3:12 it must mean God the Father). Since pagans also called their gods "lord" (1 Cor. 8:5), it is easy to see that the application of this title to Jesus held deep significance for both Jews and Gentiles.

What follows is densely packed. Peter tells us that God is merciful (1:3), about which he will be more specific in 2:10. Our salvation is of God, not of ourselves. That essential fact is also brought out by what God in His mercy gives us: a new birth. No one can be born through his own effort; for the miracle of our birth, we are totally dependent upon our parents. And so it is when we are born a second time.

The Old Testament never speaks of the new birth, but 1 Peter mentions it twice, here and in 1:23. Jesus spoke of it in John 3:3-7, and 1 John 5:1 reminds us that it is God who gives birth to the twice-born.

This new birth brings with it "a living hope," which was made possible by Christ's resurrection from the dead. A living hope could mean "a hope of life," which would make sense here, but it probably means "a dependably sure hope." This phrase is one of three in 1:3-5 beginning with the Greek preposition *eis* (translated in the NIV as "into" the first two times, and "until" the last time): (1) *living hope* through the resurrection of Jesus Christ from the dead; (2) *inheritance* that can never perish, spoil, or fade; (3) *salvation* that is ready to be revealed in the last time. (The NIV supplies the words *coming of* in verse 5 and articles in all three instances, though these words are lacking in Greek.) All three of these phrases are parallel and closely related, meaning various aspects of the same future event.

Conversion and baptism do not bring immediate enjoyment of our blessed destiny as Christians. Ours is a future hope, but not a forlorn hope; it is a living hope that affects our existence even now. Though it focuses on something in the future, it helps us to live today. We can hardly live without hope. Hebrews 6:19 calls this hope a "firm and secure" "anchor for the soul."

The dependability of this hope is tied to the resurrection of Jesus (1:3). There is no news in history more sensational than the claim that Jesus rose from the dead. If this historic claim is true, it means everything; for it means that death and the grave have been conquered, and we, too, can be victorious over them. "Because I live," said Jesus, "you also will live" (John 14:19). "Do not be afraid. I am the First and the Last. I am the Living One; I was dead, and behold I am alive for ever and ever! And I hold the keys of death and Hades" (Rev. 1:18, 19). Peter says the same thing in 1:21.

Another result of being born again is that we shall receive an inheritance that is presently kept secure for us in heaven (1:4). In the Old Testament, the inheritance of God's people was Canaan (Deut. 15:4), but what is the inheritance promised in the New Testament? We shall inherit the kingdom (Matt. 25:34; 1 Cor. 6:9, 10; 15:50;

etc.), the earth (Matt. 5:5), eternal life (Matt. 19:29, etc.), the promise (Heb. 6:12), incorruption (1 Cor. 15:50), and blessing (1 Pet. 3:9). Unlike an earthly inheritance, the one kept in heaven's bank is safe and imperishable (Matt. 6:19, 20). It will be there when the time comes for us to receive it (see also Col. 1:5).

Note that at this point (the end of verse 4) Peter changes from "us" to "you," anticipating the shift to a preaching mode, which he will continue to the end of the letter, except for 5:11.

When Peter said that his readers are guarded by God's power through faith unto "the salvation that is ready to be revealed in the last time" (1:5), it may have sounded ironic to them, considering the trouble they were getting into. But God's protection depended on their faithfulness, which is a shield (Eph. 6:16). Hostile people might afflict their bodies, but as long as they clung to God, their souls were safe (Matt. 10:28), and they could look forward to the final deliverance when their Lord returned. That is what salvation means here; it is salvation in the future tense. Various aspects of salvation operate in three tenses—the past, present, and future. God *saved us* from the penalty of sin when Jesus died and we accepted His sacrifice; He *is saving us* now from the power of sin as we depend upon Him and are faithful to Him; and He *will save us* finally from all evil at the end of time, when the Lord will come again. You can feel secure when you know that everything will come out all right in the end.

This third aspect of salvation—salvation from all evil—was already prepared to be revealed (1:5). It is clear from Peter's language that he was expecting it soon (4:7). That indeed should be the expectation of God's people in every generation.

Never Mind the Trials—Rejoice in the Salvation!

Realizing the irony, Peter anticipates the possible complaint of his readers, "That is all well and good, but why does not God protect us now?" In 1:6-9 Peter speaks of the rejoicing of believers in times of trial and danger, a rejoicing made possible by their love for Christ and by the Christian perspective.

Verse 6 is hard to translate, especially because the first phrase can be taken in several ways. Literally, it reads something like this: "In which/whom you rejoice [also could be imperative], a little while [or "a little bit"] now if it is necessary having been bothered by various trials." To what does "which/whom" (NIV, "this") refer? There are four possibilities: (1) God the Father, (2) our Lord Jesus Christ, (3) His great mercy, (4) the last time. Ramsey Michaels (*1 Peter*, 25-28) wants to understand the verb *rejoice* as having a future meaning, even though it is present tense, so that the sentence means "In the last time you will rejoice." But it is possible to have joy even in the midst of present trials, as James 1:2-4 tells us, a thought not very different from what Peter is saying here and in 4:13.

The word translated "trials" (*peirasmois*), 1:6, can mean either "temptation" or "testing." It clearly has the second meaning here. Verse 7 tells us that tests purify our faith as fire purifies gold and proves its genuineness. (Even in Eden there was a test!) Further, when you have come through the testing, you will be rewarded with "praise, glory and honor" (vs. 7). Peter is saying: "Rejoice, because though you have some trouble now, it will not last long, and it does not compare to the prize you can look forward to."

Loving the Unseen One

Peter has spoken of their faith and hope; now, in verse 8, he speaks of their love, as well as their faith. Peter was an eyewitness of the Lord Jesus (5:1; compare Acts 2:32), but the people Peter was writing to had never seen Jesus with their physical eyes. They knew about Him only through the witness of the apostles, and they could see Him only with the eye of faith. Yet that was enough for them to love and trust Him. As Jesus told Thomas, "Blessed are those who have not seen and yet have believed" (John 20:29). It was just as hard for people then to believe in God and Christ without seeing as it is now, so the apostles often had to emphasize that they had seen and touched and heard Him. (Besides the texts already mentioned, see Luke 1:2; John 1:14; 1 Cor. 9:1; 15:5; 1 John 1:1-3.)

There was another dimension to the problem in the case of the pagan Gentiles. They were accustomed to seeing their gods. They worshiped visible idols. When a pagan visited a meeting for Christian worship, his first impression was that Christians were atheists, that they had no god. For when he entered a temple of Zeus or Artemis or Hermes, there was the god; but when he came into church and looked where the god should have been, there was nothing! For the ancient pagans, seeing was believing, and so they craved idols.

These Christians loved and believed in Jesus, whom they could not now see, so they could be filled with indescribable joy, because they were winning the goal of their faith, the salvation of their souls (1:9). *Souls* (*psychōn*) here means "lives," as it does in Mark 8:34, 35 and its parallels: "If anyone would come after me, he must deny himself and take up his cross and follow me. For whoever wants to save his life [soul] will lose it, but whoever loses his life [soul] for me and for the gospel will save it." As Jim Elliot, one of the five missionaries martyred by the Auca Indians, said, "He is no fool who exchanges what he cannot keep for that which he cannot lose" (Elizabeth Elliot, *Through Gates of Splendor*). This salvation, of course, is in the future when the dead are raised to life.

More Privileged Than Prophets and Angels

The next three verses (1:10-12) are remarkable. While Peter's readers may feel themselves somehow less privileged than the apostles who had seen the Lord in person, Peter reminds them that they are more privileged than the prophets and saints of the Old Testament Scriptures. The prophets searched and studied about the salvation to come without actually learning as much about it as Peter's readers knew by hindsight and by hearing the apostles' proclamation of the gospel.

It is not quite clear just how Peter means that the prophets searched and studied. Was he thinking of Daniel, who tried to understand his visions (Dan. 8:15), who knew from Jeremiah's prophecy how long the desolation of Jerusalem would last (Dan. 9:2), and who was told that some things would not be explained until the time of the end (Dan. 12:4)? But perhaps Peter is not referring only to biblical research.

What were the prophets trying to find out? God gave them revelations about the Messiah and the salvation He was going to complete, but they did not know who the Messiah would be or when He would come. Isaiah (whose prophecy Peter is going to quote) and Zechariah saw that the Saviour would suffer, but they did not know exactly how this would come to pass. So it was with all the Old Testament writers. They were like Nebuchadnezzar in Daniel chapter 2—God gave them a revelation but did not explain it. Jesus was the explanation, so the apostles and their followers knew more than the prophets of old. What the prophets looked forward to, the Christians could look back on. As Jesus said, "Blessed are the eyes that see what you see. For I tell you that many prophets and kings wanted to see what you see but did not see it, and to hear what you hear but did not hear it" (Luke 10:23, 24).

Just how did the prophets receive their revelations? Peter says that it was "the Spirit of Christ in them prewitnessing [*promartyromenon*] the sufferings of Christ and the glories afterward" (1:11, author's translation). This suggests that Christ existed before He came in the flesh and that the Holy Spirit was and is His Spirit. In John 14:17 Jesus said that He would send His Spirit to be in us, and in John 15:5 He said that He Himself will be in us. Here is a mystery that we cannot fully understand, but we can experience it. Apparently the relationship Christ and the Spirit have after His ascension is like that which They had before the Incarnation. That is why Peter can call the Holy Spirit the Spirit of Christ. Whether we say that the Spirit inspired the prophets or say that the preexistent Christ gave revelations to them, it is all one thing.

The Christians were not only more privileged than the prophets; they were even more privileged than the angels (1:12). What the angels had longed to see and know was proclaimed to the people by Spirit-filled missionaries.

In a way, every generation has an advantage over all previous generations, and the final generation will have the greatest advantage of all in respect to knowledge of how everything turns out. But alongside that is the fact that they have to live in especially perilous times. It goes with the territory. But what a salvation!

■ Getting Into the Word

1 Peter 1:13–2:10

Read this section twice. The first time through, keep asking yourself why Peter needed to say this to his readers. The second time, ask yourself what God is saying to you through these counsels. Compare another translation if you have one. Then give attention to the following points.

1. How is this section related to the previous one? (Note the word *therefore*. Whenever you see that word, find out what it is there for!)
2. List all the metaphors and what they stand for.
3. List all the Old Testament quotations and allusions, referring to the marginal references in your Bible. Look up their original context in the Old Testament.
4. List all the imperatives—the things Peter says to do. Note any reasons given for doing them.
5. What clues are there in this section regarding the background from which Peter's readers have come? How has their status changed? In what ways have they not yet fully emerged from their former condition? (Remember the principle of "Don't put beans up your nose"!)
6. List all the things this section says about Christ.
7. List all the things this section says about the church. Are Peter's teachings in 2:4-8 related to Christ's words in Matthew 16:16-23? If so, in what way?

■ Exploring the Word

Be Holy and Live Like What You Are

By the word *therefore* (1:13), Peter tells his readers that what he has said so far is the reason for what he is going to say next. It is like the *therefore* in Romans 12:1. Privileges entail responsibilities. The great salvation God has provided for us in Christ has consequences and calls for a response. The call for response takes the form of a series of imperatives, many of them expressed somewhat strangely in Greek by participles, which may reflect a Jewish way of expression (Daube, 467-488).

The first imperative has been robbed of its color in the NIV. It literally says, "Gird up the loins of your minds" (1:13). "Gird up your loins" (or its equivalent in the NIV) is a frequent expression in the Old Testament (Job 38:3, KJV; 2 Kings 9:1, KJV). People in those days wore long robes and tunics, so when they needed to go into action, they tucked the hem of their garments up and around their belts. The expression meant "get ready for action." Since we wear trousers, we might say "roll up your sleeves" or "get with it!" But here the metaphor refers to intellectual effort: "Gird up the loins *of your mind.*" This expression should put us on notice to expect a string of some very strenuous demands.

This expression brought something else to mind. The Israelites ate the Passover with their loins girded when they were about to leave Egypt (Exod. 12:11). For Christians, Passover was Easter time. The ancient word for Easter was *Pascha*, the Aramaic word for the Passover, and it was celebrated not on Sunday but on the fourteenth day of the Jewish month of Nisan, the date of Passover, whatever day of the week that might fall on. In many early Christian communities, it was the custom to perform baptisms at that time. So baptism, Easter, and Passover were all associated. Furthermore, the Exodus of Israel from Egypt was thought of as a type or symbol of the Christian's departure from the sinful world and paganism. Egypt was a symbol of these things, going back to the prologue to the Ten Commandments: "I am the Lord thy God, who brought you out of the land of Egypt, out of the house of bondage" (Exod. 20:2, RSV). Also remember that in 1 Corinthians 10:1, 2, Paul equates Israel's miraculous passage through the Red Sea with baptism: "Our forefathers were all under the cloud and . . . they all passed through the sea. They were all baptized into Moses in the cloud and in the sea." For such reasons some scholars argue that most of Peter's following words are part of the admonition that was given to baptismal candidates. Perhaps it would be safer to say simply that these words *recall* the admonition given to baptismal candidates.

In the NIV, the next imperative is "be self-controlled." The Greek can mean either "be sober" or "pay attention." If the second meaning is the one intended, then it simply reinforces the first imperative. While Christians certainly should not get literally drunk, the more insidious problem is spiritual stupor, mental and moral drowsiness. Peter is going to repeat this thought in 4:7 and 5:8.

Next, he says to "set your hope completely on the grace brought to you by the revelation of Jesus Christ" (1:13, my translation). This grace is, of course, another word for the future salvation described in the previous section, the time when Jesus comes again. The point is that we are not to have alternative hopes, reservations, or hesitations. You bet your whole wad on this one!

Verse 14 is a strong clue that Peter's readers were formerly pagans. The Bible and Jewish literature often emphasized that the heathen lived in ignorance, resulting in idolatry and immorality (e.g., Acts 17:30). But they have been figuratively called out of "Egypt," called to leave their old habits and customs, called to be holy, as God is holy (1:16). Holiness is specialness and separateness, with moral consequences. Peter quotes Leviticus 19:2, which occurs in what scholars call the Holiness Code (Leviticus 17 through 26). That code warned: "You must not do as they do in Egypt, where you used to live" (Lev. 18:3). By applying these ideas to his readers, Peter is saying that though they may have been Gentiles, they have now become the new Israelites, a concept he had introduced in 1:1, 2 and to which he will return. Their "holiness code" is the teachings and example of Jesus. Ellen White explains holiness this way:

> Holiness is agreement with God. By sin the image of God in man has been marred and well-nigh obliterated; it is the work of the gospel to restore that which has been lost; and we are to co-operate with the divine agency in this work. And how can we come into harmony with God, how shall we receive His likeness, unless we obtain a knowledge of Him? It is this knowledge that Christ came into the world to reveal unto us (White, *Testimonies for the Church*, 5:743).

Bought With an Imperishable Price

In the next few verses (1:17-21), Peter points out that Christian holiness is based on Christ's death and exaltation. But Peter first reminds his readers that they have received the privilege of calling upon God as "Father." They can pray, "Our Father which art in heaven" (Matt. 6:9, KJV) and even address Him as *Abba* (Rom. 8:15; Gal. 4:6), just as Jesus did (Mark 14:36). *Abba* was a term expressive of intimate relationship, but such familiarity does not make God any less awesome. God is still the impartial Judge (1:17).

This is a balanced and true picture of God. People tend to go to extremes in their thinking about God. Formerly, many people thought of Him as aloof and harshly judgmental. In our day, people think of Him as a friend on more or less equal terms with themselves, an indulgent and democratic modern daddy. But God is neither, or He is both. He is a loving Father, but He is also an impartial Judge. You cannot love a God whom you do not respect.

Peter reminds his readers again that they are but pilgrims passing through this world and tells them that in view of God's impartial judgment, they should conduct themselves "in reverent fear" (1:17). This word *fear* is prominent in the letter (2:17; 3:6, 14). It means awe, not terror. Perhaps a secular equivalent today would be a sense of respect for lawful authority and a sense of accountability; if more people had it, we would all feel safer. But if you stick your tongue out at God, you won't get away with it.

The real motivation for upright conduct during our pilgrimage here comes out in the following verses (1:18-21). It is the realization of how great a price God paid for our redemption—"the precious blood of Christ" (1:19). Peter is reminding his readers; he says "you know" this (1:18). In fact, these verses were full of familiar teachings, and we find many of the same phrases elsewhere in the New Testament (e.g., Titus 2:12-14).

They are familiar to us, too, and because of that familiarity, they may not strike us with the force that they should. We might begin to realize some of the original impact if we exercise our historical imagination and think about what the words meant when Peter was writing them. Peter tells his readers that they were "redeemed" or "ransomed," RSV (Greek *elytrōthēte*), from the vain customs and habits handed down from their ancestors (1:18).

Ransom was a word that rang bells for both Gentile and Jew. The Gentile would have thought first of the slave markets. A large proportion of the population of the Roman Empire was slaves, and many of the church members were slaves. A person could become a slave in many ways. His city or army might have been conquered in war. He may have been on a ship captured by pirates. He may have fallen into debt that he could not pay. He or she might even have been born into slavery. Such a person was bought or sold as chattel, auctioned at one of the slave markets. The biggest market was on the island of Delos, where hundreds of men and women were exhibited naked and sold off every day. Educated Greeks fetched the best price, for they were useful as bookkeepers and secretaries. They were usually treated well and could even own slaves of their own! Others might not be treated so well. A mistress might scratch out a slave girl's eyes if, while styling her owner's hair, the slave got a curl out of place.

There were opponents of slavery in those days, and some philanthropist might buy a slave's freedom, or a free relative or religious foundation might do it. Jews generally tried hard to obtain the freedom of their countrymen, so few Jews remained slaves very long. The ransom money was called *lytron*, and the act of ransoming or redeeming was called *lytrōsis* or *apolytrōsis*.

A Jew hearing or using this word could have thought of many things—the ransoming of alienated land before the Jubilee year (Lev. 25:25-28) or the half-shekel temple tax (Exod. 30:12), but especially he would have thought of the deliverance from Egyptian bondage.

In the case of Gentiles and also in some of the Jewish cases, the redemption was effected through the payment of money—of gold and silver. But the redemption from inherited and cultivated sin that Christians enjoy was not bought with gold and silver but with Christ's precious blood (1:18, 19). The ransom language applied to Christ's work probably goes back to His saying in Mark 10:45: "The Son of Man did not come to be served, but to serve, and to give his life as a ransom for many." Verse 19 compares the blood of Christ to that of a sacrificial lamb, unblemished (Lev. 22:17-25). These words strongly suggest that Jesus was free from the stain of sin. Note that Jesus did not just *pay* the price; He *was* the price. "Look, the Lamb of God, who takes away the sin of the world!" (John 1:29).

Jesus Himself knew what the plan was (Mark 8:31). Peter tells us that the plan of redemption and the sacrifice was in God's mind "before the creation of the world, but was revealed in these last times for your sake" (1:20). The Greek literally says it "was made manifest at the end of the time periods [*chronōn*] for your sakes." The early church felt that the final epoch of world history began with Christ's first coming (Heb. 1:2; 1 Cor. 10:11).

Peter says Christ originated the faith of the believers (1:21). His language is ambiguous; it is not clear whether he means that through Christ they could believe in God or that because of Christ they could have confidence in God. Perhaps both ideas are true. This harks back to the point made in 1:3.

The God who raised Christ from the dead also glorified Him (vs. 21). The glorification of Christ is described at greater length in Philippians 2:9-11. Notice what Jesus prayed in John 17:5: "And now, Father, glorify me in your presence with the glory I had with you before the world began."

Born of Imperishable Seed

In 1:22-25 Peter speaks of one of the fruits of the Christian's obedience: love of the brethren, based on the new birth engendered by the living Word of God. The Greek of verses 22 and 23 literally reads: "Having cleansed yourselves by the obedience of the truth for an unhypocritical love of the brethren, love one another to the maximum from the heart, having been born again, not of perishable sperm but of imperishable, through the living and abiding Word of God."

The purifying or cleansing may refer to baptism, and the truth being obeyed was the gospel. By this we become children of God, and every child of God is our brother or sister. "Everyone who believes that Jesus is the Christ is born of God, and everyone who loves the father loves his child as well" (1 John 5:1). Whenever the word *unhypocritical* (*anypokritos*, translated as "sincere" by the NIV) is used in the New Testament, it is related to love (Rom. 12:9; 2 Cor. 6:6; 1 Tim. 1:5; 2 Tim. 1:5; James 3:17; and here). The word for brotherly love is *philadelphia*, and Peter will mention it again in 2 Peter 1:7.

What is the opposite of unhypocritical love? Is there such a thing as pretended love? What Peter tells his readers here must have been a hard saying. It is hard for *us*, because—to be honest—it is not always easy to love some of our brothers and sisters. Family fights are the worst kind, and some of the bitterest animosity arises between church members, because when there is a difference of opinion in the church, you cannot just walk away from it without walking away from the church. We are often not content just to say, "You're wrong!" In the church we say, "You're a heretic," or, "You're an agent of Satan." To make things even more complicated, there actually *are* such things as heretics and agents of Satan, as we will see in 2 Peter and Jude. But here is a good rule to follow in church disputes, whether about doctrine or policy: When two people of good will and equal learning cannot agree about some point, the reason must be that the information or evidence is ambiguous or insufficient to lead to a clear conclusion. No such point should be made a test of fellowship. In such cases, fellowship is more needful than agreement.

Still, what if you just don't *like* a fellow believer? It may help to realize that real *agapē*-love is not so much something you feel as something you do. Sincere love is simply treating people right, whether you "like" them or not, whether you "feel" like it or not. You may not always like your fleshly siblings, either, but God forbid that you should cause them harm.

Just as we gain siblings by natural birth, we gain even dearer siblings by supernatural birth. The idea expressed in verse 23 is similar to that in John 1:12, 13. Those who believe in Jesus become children of God—"children born not of bloods [see note in NIV], nor of human decision or a husband's will, but born of God." The plural "bloods" in John 1:13 refers to the genetic material from the two human parents. Peter says the imperishable sperm (or seed) is the Word of God, just as Jesus said in Luke's report of the parable of the sower, "The seed is the word of God" (Luke 8:11; compare James 1:18). The *Word* specifically means "the gospel"—first the message of Jesus; then the message about Jesus. Peter ends this passage with his second Bible quotation, from Isaiah 40:6-8, which contrasts the perishability of flesh with the permanence of the word of the Lord, and Peter concludes by declaring: That word is the gospel we preached to you (1:24, 25).

Peter keeps hammering home these truths in 2:1-3, developing the metaphor of new birth. "Therefore," he begins and goes on to lay down two imperatives with the verbs "rid yourselves" and "crave." If Christians have purified themselves and become obedient children, what then? New birth should result in new life.

The word *rid* in Greek (2:1) means "to strip off," as in stripping off one's garments. This may refer to an ancient Christian baptismal practice. As early catacomb paintings and references in the writings of the ancient church fathers (e.g., Hippolytus, *Apostolic Traditions*, 21) indicate, people stripped off all their clothing when they were baptized. (That is still the practice in Jewish proselyte baptism.) They stripped off their old clothes before immersing themselves and then put on brand-new clothes afterward. That was symbolic of putting off the old life and putting on the new life of Jesus Christ. There are five other places in the New Testament where we find expressions like this (Rom. 13:12; Eph. 4:22, 25; Col. 3:8; James 1:21), but it is not certain whether these references reflected this practice or prompted it.

Most of these passages say to put off virtually the same kinds of vices. For example, Colossians 3:8-10, says:

> Now you must rid yourselves of [literally, "strip off"] all such things as these: anger, rage, malice, slander, and filthy language from your lips. Do not lie to each other, since you have taken off your old self with its practices and have put on the new self, which is being renewed in knowledge in the image of its Creator.

You can imagine that it was an impressive thing when a baptismal candidate removed his clothing while an elder charged him, "Take off all badness and all deceit and hypocrisy and jealousy and all slander." Then after the immersion the elder would have said, "Put on Jesus Christ," as the candidate put on his brand-new garments.

Lists of vices such as that in 2:1 were common in the moral literature of the time, and there are many of them in the New Testament (Matt. 15:19 and parallels; Luke 18:11; Rom. 1:29-31; 13:13; 1 Cor. 5:10, 11; 6:9, 10; 2 Cor. 12:20; Gal. 5:19-21; Eph. 4:31; 5:3-5; Col. 3:5, 8; 1 Tim. 1:9; 6:4, 5; Titus 3:3; 1 Pet. 2:1; 4:3; Rev. 9:21; 21:8; 22:15). The vices mentioned in 1 Peter 2:1 are those which are especially likely to sour relationships in the church.

In 2:2 Peter switches to another metaphor that some scholars also connect with ancient baptismal customs, the custom of giving the newly baptized persons a taste of milk and honey, a symbol of the heavenly Canaan, of which they had now become citizens. (Exodus 3:8 calls Canaan a "land flowing with milk and honey.") But the earliest evidence for that custom is from the end of the second century. Peter does not mention honey, and it is clear that he does not mean literal milk. The readers are to crave "spiritual milk." The word *spiritual* (NIV) is literally *reasonable* or *logical* (*logikos*) in Greek (the same word used in Romans 12:1, which speaks of "your spiritual worship"); it means the opposite of literal or physical.

By using this metaphor of God's milk, a feminine aspect, Peter balances his earlier metaphor of God's seed in 1:23. By being born again (1:23), we become newborn babies (2:2) and need the nourishment of the milk of God's life-giving goodness communicated to us by His Word, the gospel. A physically newborn infant naturally craves the milk from his mother's breast, but Peter has to command us to crave the "pure spiritual milk." The result of drinking it in is that we grow up into salvation, which shows that we do not simply wait passively for our future deliverance. The word *pure* literally means "without deceit," deceit being one of the vices Peter tells us to get rid of in verse 1, thus tying the two verses together. We who have received the milk of divine kindness will dispense the milk of human kindness.

Peter says that his readers have already tasted that the Lord is delicious (2:3). This is a clear allusion to Psalm 34:8, "Taste and see that the Lord is good." Peter is fond of that Psalm and quotes from it again in 3:10-12. The tasting took place when they were baptized, and the Lord is Jesus Christ.

The picture here is of a newborn baby who just wants to suck and suck. Peter is telling us that we should have that kind of suction for the things of the Lord. But first we must have an appetite, and a dead person has no appetite. That is why those who are dead in their sins must be born again. Sometimes our trouble is that we try to preach *re*vival to people who have not yet been "vived"! It is like going into the morgue and serving a banquet to the corpses—then afterward haranguing them and telling them to get up and do calisthenics! The sign of spiritual life is spiritual appetite.

The Stone and the Stones

In 2:4-10 Peter suddenly moves into the topic of ecclesiology, which is the doctrine of the church. Christians are not just born-again individuals, but parts of a larger whole. When people come to Christ, they come to the church. But Peter's ecclesiology is based on Christology, the doctrine of Christ. Christians are what they are because Christ is what He is. Peter piles up many metaphors that are sometimes hard to unscramble, but it all centers around three more Bible quotations (Isaiah 28:16; Psalm 118:22; and Isaiah 8:14, in that order) that were important for early Christians. These three quotations all contain the Greek word *lithos*, a root that occurs in English words such as *lithograph* and *monolith*. *Lithos* means a stone that has been squared and dressed for use in masonry, unlike a natural rock (*petra* or *petros*). It is no coincidence that Peter calls both Christ and the Christians stones.

Verse 4 shows that the delicious Lord whom Peter mentioned in verse 3 is in fact Jesus Christ. He calls him the living Stone. "Living" not only indicates that Peter does not mean a literal stone, but it shows that he is talking about the resurrected Jesus (compare "the living word" in 1:23), the source of the living hope (1:3). Anticipating his quotations in reverse order, first, Psalm 118:22 and then

Isaiah 28:16, Peter points out that Christ was rejected by men, just as were his readers who follow Christ's pattern. But like Christ, His followers are chosen by God and precious in His sight. The "men" who rejected Christ are all unbelievers, both Jews and Gentiles.

Verse 5 drives home the fact that Christians are also living stones, drawing out the parallel between their experience and Christ's. By faith they are merged with Him (like branches attached to the real Vine, as John 15 tells us; but instead of that botanical metaphor, Peter uses an architectural one). It is not surprising, then, that unbelievers will treat them just as they treated Jesus. Peter is thinking of all enemies of God's people, but especially their pagan neighbors and townspeople, for here, again, he describes Christian believers as Israelites, the chosen people—a theme he will develop further in 2:9, 10.

The stones are being built into a spiritual temple—the text says "house," but a house where priests offer sacrifices is a temple, a metaphor that Paul also uses (1 Cor. 3:16, 17). The church is the temple, and it is also the priesthood that serves in the temple (compare 2:9), "offering spiritual sacrifices acceptable to God through Jesus Christ" (vs. 5). Just as the temple is spiritual, so are the sacrifices spiritual, not physical—in contrast to both the pagan temples and the Jerusalem temple.

What are the spiritual sacrifices offered in the church? Can anything be added to the sacrifice that Jesus offered, both as Victim and as Priest? According to Romans 12:1, we offer our bodies, meaning our very selves; Ephesians 5:2 tells us that our fragrant offering is a life of love; and Hebrews 13:15, 16 informs us that it is praise ("the fruit of the lips") and doing good. In a word, our offering to God, made acceptable by the merits of Jesus Christ, consists of worshipful prayer and good works. What kind of good works? This letter describes them: a life of unselfish conduct. That was the rhythm of Christ's life, to be imitated by those who follow Him: alternation between mountain and multitude, between the vertical relationship to God and the horizontal relationship to our fellow human beings, between worship and service.

This is not easy to do alone, and God does not want us to do it alone. That is why the living stones are fitted together into a house of God. Ellen White's comment is appropriate:

> The Jewish temple was built of hewn stones quarried out of the mountains; and every stone was fitted for its place in the temple, hewed, polished, and tested before it was brought to Jerusalem. And when all were brought to the ground, the building went together without the sound of ax or hammer. This building represents God's spiritual temple, which is composed of material gathered out of every nation, and tongue, and people, of all grades, high and low, rich and poor, learned and unlearned. These are not dead substances to be fitted by hammer and chisel. They are living stones, quarried out from the world by the truth; and the great Master Builder, the Lord of the temple, is now hewing and polishing them, and fitting them for their respective places in the spiritual temple. When completed, this temple will be perfect in all its parts, the admiration of angels and of men; for its Builder and Maker is God.
>
> Let no one think that there need not be a stroke placed upon him. There is no person, no nation, that is perfect in every habit and thought. One must learn of another. Therefore God wants the different nationalities to mingle together, to be one in judgment, one in purpose. Then the union that there is in Christ will be exemplified (White, *Testimonies for the Church*, 9:180, 181).

Peter has now pretty well laid out what he wants us to get out of Isaiah 28:16 and Psalm 118:22 (which he now quotes in 2:6, 7) except for one more point—the contrast between believers and unbelievers. Believers will be vindicated, but unbelievers who have rejected both the stones and Christ, the Stone, will stumble and fall, as the quotation of Isaiah 8:14 in verse 8 brings out. Psalm 118:22 was a favorite verse among early Christians, for Christ had applied it to Himself and the Jewish leaders (Mark 12:10 and parallels). Peter himself had applied it to the Sanhedrin (Acts 4:11), but here he applies it to the citizens and officials of Gentile society.

The last part of verse 8 is easily misunderstood, for it seems to teach the doctrine of double predestination, that God destines some for perdition as well as some for salvation. The question is: What were the unbelievers destined for, stumbling or disobedience? "They stumble because they disobey the message." Disobeying the message means not accepting the gospel of Christ. That is a choice, but when people make that choice, the consequence of ultimate ruin is inevitable, for it is the will of God. "This does not mean that God has appointed men to disobedience, but that He has foreordained stumbling to be the punishment of disobedience" (Vaughan and Lea, 47). Stumbling and falling are the opposite of the vindication and honor that will be the destiny of believers.

The Stone that is precious to some is a stumbling block to others. The Word of God is never without effect: it either softens or hardens. We cannot be unaffected by it. "So," says God, "is my word that goes out from my mouth: It will not return to me empty, but will accomplish what I desire and achieve the purpose for which I sent it" (Isaiah 55:11). That is why no one should ever speak—or listen to—God's message lightly or carelessly.

At the end of this section (2:9, 10), Peter sums up and develops some of the key points he has made. In contrast to unbelievers, believers have an exalted calling. Peter heaps up words for them in verse 9, all drawn from the Old Testament.

They are "a chosen people." Peter has said this many times, thus declaring them to be the new Israel.

They are "a royal priesthood" (some would translate it "a royal house, a priesthood"), a phrase taken from Exodus 19:6 and also quoted in Revelation 1:6 and 5:10. It is important to note that this title applies to the church corporately, not to individuals as priests.

They are "a holy nation" (also from Exod. 19:6). They make up a new nation, a nationality that supersedes any other ethnic identity.

They are "a people belonging to God." This is a phrase that the KJV translates "a peculiar people," but the word *peculiar* meant something quite different in 1611 than it means now! The phrase comes from Isaiah 43:21, "The people I formed for myself that they may proclaim my praise." Peter takes his cue from that and adds to it. The purpose of this glorious calling is that we are to proclaim the wonderful deeds of Him who called us. For the ancient Israelites, God's wonderful deed was the deliverance from Egyptian bondage, especially the passage through the sea. For Christians, it is the death and resurrection of Jesus Christ, in whom we have eternal life. Israelites proclaimed God's miraculous work when they celebrated Passover. In the Lord's Supper, Christians proclaim the Lord's death until He comes. We are also to witness to the Gentiles, as God had intended the Israelites to do. Our proclamation is both internal and external. There is no better way to witness than to tell what the Lord has done for you.

Verse 10 sounds poetic: "Once you were not a people, / but now you are the people of God; / once you had not received mercy, / but now you have received mercy." It may very well be a verse from an early Christian hymn based on Hosea 1:6-10 and 2:23. There is also something like it in Romans 9:25, 26. It was quite natural to see in those passages from Hosea a reference to receiving Gentiles into the new Israel. *People* generally meant "Israel"; the Gentiles were "the nations."

Peter has now placed before his troubled readers a great destiny, which they will share with their Lord. He has indicated that their privilege brings with it the obligation to conduct themselves like the holy people they are. Finally, he has shown them the contrast between their position as believers and that of the unbelievers who are troubling them. The next item on his agenda is to give them practical instruction about how to relate to the people of unbelieving society as well as to fellow believers in the church.

∎ Applying the Word

1 Peter 1:3–2:10

1. **How is it possible for me to have peace with God and with myself and yet be on my toes spiritually, as 1 Peter 1:13 calls for?**
2. **How can I know that I have been born again? (Hint: Read**

through 1 John.) In what ways will my new birth be demonstrated in daily life? (See John 3:8.)

3. How is it possible to love someone I have never seen? What do I mean when I say that I love God? How is my love for God different from my love for a family member or close friend? How is it similar?

4. Believing without seeing is hard for modern people too. What are our idols?

5. In what ways am I more privileged than the people who saw Jesus in person?

6. What do I think of this statement by one commentator (Reicke, 84): "Holiness is not an attribute of man, and man cannot attain it by himself, nor progressively sanctify himself, and then triumphantly present the result to God. Rather, holiness belongs to God; He is the only Holy One. Inasmuch as He is holy, His people must live a holy life before Him. This God-centered doctrine of sanctification differs from the view that man, through holy living, can develop a holy personality"? How would I define holiness? What specific attributes would I need to change in my life in order for me to demonstrate holiness in my character? To what extent should I depend on God for holiness, and what part do I play?

7. How is my concept of God influenced by ideas prevailing in my culture? In what ways does modern culture make it difficult for me to understand the biblical pictures of God? Might contemporary culture in the first century have affected the New Testament writers' concepts of God? In what ways?

8. What kind of idols do modern people make in seeking to make the unseen Lord visible?

9. How can we reconcile the view of the early church that Christ was made manifest in the last time with our view that there have been several time periods marked out by Daniel's prophecies for the time after the first coming of Christ?

10. Can there be such a thing as pretended love? If so, what would its effects be?

11. Do we ever outgrow our appetite and need for the milk of God's Word? How can I explain what is said in 1 Corinthians 3:2 and Hebrews 5:12?

12. How can I show my appreciation for being one of God's chosen people?

■ Researching the Word

1. Look up the original contexts of all the Old Testament texts that Peter has quoted in this section, and write down anything that strikes you about how Peter has applied them. (Note that most of the quotations in 1 Peter are based on the Greek translation of the Old Testament, known as the Septuagint, but our English translations of the Old Testament are usually based on the Hebrew text. This explains some differences of wording.)

2. Using an exhaustive concordance, look up all the occurrences of the word *holy*, and make a notation for each one about what it is that is called holy. What do you conclude about the meaning of holiness?

3. Look up all the texts that have vice lists, and collate them (see the list on page 63). What vices are most often mentioned? Why?

■ Further Study of the Word

1. In John 3:10 Jesus chided Nicodemus for not knowing about the new birth, though he was a teacher in Israel. Since the new birth is not mentioned in the Old Testament, why should Nicodemus have known about it? To learn about the idea of being born again in rabbinic Judaism, read G. F. Moore, *Judaism in the First Centuries of the Christian Era: The Age of the Tannaim*, 1:323-335.

2. For the issue of God's foreknowledge and predestination,

see G. W. Bromiley, ed., *The International Standard Bible Encyclopedia*, 3:945-951.

3. For further study on the dimensions of salvation in the Bible, see the article on salvation by A. Richardson in G. A. Buttrick, ed., *The Interpreter's Dictionary of the Bible*, 4:168-181.

4. For a thorough study of the New Testament metaphors for the church, see P. S. Minear, *Images of the Church in the New Testament*. The high points of this book are summarized in part of Minear's article on the church in G. A. Buttrick, ed., *The Interpreter's Dictionary of the Bible*, 1:609-616.

CHAPTER THREE

Being Good People in a Bad World

1 Peter 2:11–4:11

Having laid a firm theological foundation for what he is about to say, Peter now addresses his readers again as "Dear Friends" (literally, "Beloved") (2:11), takes a breath, and heads into very practical matters that are the real concern of the letter. The issue is: How are Christians to conduct themselves as members of a society that is rejecting them? How are they to relate to unbelievers and their expectations, and for that matter, to fellow believers? What is their controlling motive in these relationships? These issues bring us into the heart of the letter.

The first two verses of this part of the letter (2:11, 12) lay down its basic idea, first negatively (vs. 11) and then positively (vs. 12). On the one hand, the believers are like foreigners in the land who do not conform to the sinful pagan customs and ways that they once followed. On the other hand, there are other expectations and moral standards of non-Christian society with which they should conform, so that the nasty rumors may be proved false.

After stating the basic principle thus, Peter proceeds to show how it applies to various specific relationships and roles in society. He discusses submission to various authorities and institutions (vss. 13-17), submission of slaves to masters (vss. 18-25), submission of wives to husbands (3:1-6), relation of husbands to wives (vs. 7), and finally, a summary of the foregoing that calls for harmony in such a way that it could also apply to relationships within the Christian brotherhood (vss. 8-12). All this follows a literary form found in both Christian and non-Christian moral literature; scholars call such lists of roles and duties "domestic codes" or "household duty codes."

At 3:13 Peter leaves ethical specifics and deals at length with the special *Christian motivation for moral living and confidence in suffering, a subject that he has already touched upon profoundly in 2:21-25 while instructing slaves. Verses 13 to 17 are closely tied to the domestic code by the repetition of six key words and themes: suffering, doing good, doing evil, slander, justice, and the will of God (Balch, 125 to 126). Above all, Peter holds up the example of the suffering Christ, whose victory gives confidence to people who suffer for Him (3:18–4:6). Warning his readers (and hearers—the letter was to be read in church) once more against the dissipated lifestyle and practices of unbelievers, Peter reminds them of the coming judgment.*

Our passage concludes with some additional specific counsels about relationships within the church and ends with a doxology (4:7-11).

■ Getting Into the Word

1 Peter 2:11–3:12

Read through 1 Peter 2:11 to 4:11 to get the sweep of the argument, and then concentrate on reading 2:11 to 3:12. If you have more than one translation, compare them. Then attend to these points:

1. Why is Peter concerned about the various relationships he deals with in this passage? Why might Christians behave differently from the way Peter prescribes? What do you think is the background of 2:16?

2. Do you think that the social and moral standards Peter lays down here were uniquely Christian standards or that they were mostly standards shared with non-Christian society? How does 2:12, 15 help to answer that question?

3. How would you describe the way Peter wants Christians to relate to the outside world? To fellow believers?

4. List all the places where Peter uses the words *submit* and *submissive*. With the help of a concordance, find other places in the New Testament where these words are used. Summarize your findings in your notebook.

5. If we did not have the four Gospels, what could we know

about the life and teachings of Jesus just from this passage?

6. With the help of your Bible's margin or notes, list all the quotations and allusions to the Old Testament that you can find in this passage; then compare them to the original words in the Old Testament. What differences in wording do you find? (Keep in mind that Peter mostly quotes from the ancient Greek translation of the Old Testament, called the Septuagint, while our English translations are mostly made from the standard Hebrew text, called the Masoretic text.)

7. As we have noted, this passage largely conforms to a literary form called a household duty code or domestic code. Compare the other places in the New Testament where we find such lists of roles and duties: Ephesians 5:21 to 6:9; Colossians 3:18 to 4:1; 1 Timothy 2:8-15; 5:1, 2; 6:1, 2; Titus 2:1-10; 3:1. Note which roles are mentioned in each passage. Does 1 Peter 5:1-7 also belong among such lists? Are any roles missing in 1 Peter that were usually included? Which, and why? What does Peter include that you do not find in the others?

8. Why do you think Peter says so much more to wives than to husbands? And why does he address slaves but not masters?

9. List the specific things Peter tells each class of persons to do and the reasons he gives for doing them.

10. What two examples does Peter hold up to his readers/hearers in this passage?

■ Exploring the Word

Basic Issues

A group of people who voluntarily choose to live like aliens within the larger society would today be called a counterculture. Today, such a group might be expected to place itself in an adversarial posture toward outsiders. Katherine Kersten describes a typical contemporary movement of this nature:

It gains its sense of identity by indignantly rejecting everything the larger culture holds dear. Consumed by self-pity, the opposing self embraces "the great modern strategy of being the insulted and the injured." . . . Those who adopt the identity of the opposing self tend to be drawn to one another, forming what political scientist Paul Hollander has called the "adversary culture." By embracing utopian ideals that can never be satisfied, such people ensure that they will always have much to complain of (Kersten, 23).

That is what we might expect in the instruction that Peter sends to these early Christians—but, in fact, his advice is not so simple. Peter has plenty to warn his readers against, but we find here no whining and no blanket condemnation of the morals of the outside society. On the contrary, he admonishes his hearers to conform to many of the values and expectations of the unbelieving authorities and neighbors so as not to attract undeserved criticism against the Christian movement.

Peter begins this section, however, with a negative admonition, stressing again the alienated status of the New Israel (using the same terms that he used in 1:1, 17) and warning against "sinful [literally 'fleshly'] desires, which war against your soul" (2:11). Were these words countercultural? To that question, we cannot give a simple answer. On one hand, these words ran counter to the popular culture, but on the other hand, they were in harmony with sentiments commonly expressed by high-minded philosophers and other morally sensitive pagans and Jews of the time.

Popular culture was frankly immoral and recognized as such by the more thoughtful people. The public taste had become progressively coarser, seen in the theater and the amphitheater. Entertainment was characterized by obscenity in the theater and violence and bloodshed in the amphitheater. All this had an inevitable effect on society and religion. The popular motto was, "To step aside is human," said with a shrug (Angus, 41-50).

Suppose you were invited to a banquet. If it were a large affair, it would be held in a banqueting room connected with one of the temples, where meat offered to idols was the great delicacy. After the meal, the family women having been dismissed, came a drinking party and entertainment. The latter commonly consisted of flute-girls and *hetairae* ("companions," meaning call girls), the only women now present. Sexual relations with these women or with boys would end the evening (Witherington, 41).

Thoughtful people raised voices of protest against the social deterioration and indulgence. Though the usual Greek ideal was "moderation in all things"—even in vice—some philosophers, by way of reaction, advocated simplicity, abstemiousness, and even asceticism. Popular moralists writing and preaching about "how to live" managed to attract audiences. Their ideal was a life of self-control and quiet devotion to philosophical contemplation, which became a sort of religion for educated people. About the time Peter was writing, philosophers like Musonius, Epictetus, and Dio Chrysostom were also warning against the fleshly vices that "war against your soul."

These moralists had the attention of many in the ruling class, who were concerned about political instability and the rising crime rate. They lamented the decline from the virtuous "good old days" and the departure from ancestral traditions. They associated these problems with lessening of respect for authority and breakdown of the hierarchical social order, beginning in the home. In their view, when women, children, and slaves did not keep their proper place and submit to their husbands, parents, and masters, their insubordination undermined the strength and stability of the entire Roman Empire. They considered good domestic order essential to good civic order.

This idea that there must be a chain of command from top to bottom—something quite different from modern democratic ideas—had been stressed by the classic philosophers of several centuries earlier. According to Plato, contempt for law originated with modern music, in not being satisfied with the old style. And then . . .

> Next after this form of liberty would come that which refuses to be subject to rulers; and, following on that, the shirking of submission to one's parents and elders and their

admonitions; then, as the penultimate stage, comes the
effort to disregard the laws; while the last stage of all is to
lose all respect for oaths or pledges or divinities (Plato,
Laws, 710B, cited in Balch, 25).

Aristotle believed that when women gain power over men, the
government goes down the tubes and loses wars. Like almost all philosophers who followed him, he drew a parallel between household
order and civic order. When wives, children, and slaves are not submissive, it leads to anarchy.

What is more, many of the authorities and philosophers were convinced that much of the trouble was caused by the new religious
cults that were coming from the East and from Egypt. These included the wild cult of Dionysus and the cult of the Egyptian god-
dess Isis, both popular among women and associated with immoral
rites. Judaism was often lumped together with them, largely because
Jews made very poor slaves who refused to work on Sabbaths, eat
pork, or worship their masters' gods. The head of the household
expected everyone in his family, including women, children, and
slaves, to share in his religion. As Plutarch said, "It is becoming for a
wife to worship and know only the gods that her husband believes in,
and to shut the front door tight upon all queer rituals and outlandish
superstitions" (Plutarch, *Advice to Bride and Groom*, 140D [19]).

The rulers and citizens felt that Christianity was especially sinis-
ter. Not only did this new religion make slaves insubordinate by their
refusal to participate in their masters' religion, but it also converted
the wives and, thus, they charged, destroyed the harmony of the family. So people regarded Christianity as a threat to the very founda-
tions of society and government, turning the world upside down.

It is against this background that we can understand Peter's concerns. Not only does he want his readers to avoid the immoral conduct
that Christians were ignorantly being accused of, but he wants them to
display the kind of conduct that society regards as praiseworthy.
Self-indulgent or immoral living will not only destroy his readers' souls;
it will destroy their witness among the pagans. Even though the pagans
may themselves live self-indulgent lives, they know better.

The apostolic writers were not indifferent to the reputation Christians made among the Gentiles (see, for example, 1 Cor. 10:32; Col. 4:5; 1 Thess. 4:12; 1 Tim. 3:7; 5:14; 6:1; Titus 2:5-10; as well as 1 Pet. 3:16). It goes back to what Jesus said in the Sermon on the Mount: "Let your light shine before men, that they may see your good deeds and praise your Father in heaven" (Matt. 5:16), a saying that Peter echoes here (2:12).

What is the day of God's inspection, the day of God's visitation (vs. 12)? The term probably goes back to Isaiah 10:3 and means the judgment day. The thought must be that Christians will share, in a secondary way, the acclamation that even Christ's enemies will accord Him at the end, according to Philippians 2:10, 11. Revelation 20:11-15 graphically paints the scene.

The Christian's Social Responsibilities

Peter's command for relating to the institutions of society (2:12) is expressed in one word: *submit* (vs. 13)! The very idea is dissonant with our modern ethic of human equality and democracy, but it was in complete harmony with the moral ideas of the Roman Empire in the first century A.D. The thinking was that every individual had a definite standing in society, and that position in life carried with it clear responsibilities. In every relationship, one party was superior, and the other was inferior and subordinate. You were never long in doubt about where you stood. A new relationship was unstable until the proper "pecking order" was established. The great object in life was to acquire honor (which could be done only by taking it from someone else), but there were limits to how much a person could achieve. The general stations in life were determined by sex, age, and ownership—things that were not readily changed. You would no more think of challenging your husband, parent, or owner than you would think of adding a cubit to your height. The ancients could not conceive of any alternative system other than anarchy and chaos.

Moralists, both pagan and Jewish, often wrote about the roles and relationships that should exist in society, and especially in the household. We call these traditional formulations "domestic codes" or

"household duty codes." There are several such lists in the New Testament also (see page 75, under "Getting Into the Word"). Usually
they deal with three pairs of relationships, with one in each pair submitting to the other—wives and husbands, children and parents, slaves
and masters (e.g., Colossians 3:18–4:1). The codes describe the conduct expected of each member in each pair. But here in 1 Peter the
code is different. Peter describes the duty of slaves but not that of
masters. He says much to wives but only a little to husbands. And he
doesn't mention the parent-child relationship at all. The reason is
probably that Peter needs to deal only with those who are victims of
misunderstanding and suffering. Besides, it is likely that there were
then many more slaves and women among the believers than masters and men. Though Peter leaves out some relationships that were
usually included in the domestic codes, he alludes briefly to others in
2:13, 17.

Peter here lists those to whom Christians, as participants in human
society, must submit. "The king" (vs. 13) is the Roman emperor. At this
time, Pontus, Galatia, Cappadocia, Asia, and Bithynia were all under
the direct rule of the emperor, who was represented by governors. The
governors punished those who did evil and praised those who did good
(vs. 14), and doing good certainly included submitting. The good was
such that the pagan governor recognized it as good. The behavior demanded is not distinctively Christian, but the motive behind it is: "for
the Lord's sake" (vs. 13). It is like saying in our day: "Obey the speed
limit for the Lord's sake." This kind of doing good would refute the
charge that Christians were subversive anarchists. Christians had given
up conventional religion; should they also give up conventional morality? Peter's answer was that they should not.

Embarrassing though it must have been, there were apparently
people calling themselves Christians who gave outsiders good cause
to be suspicious that Christians were sociopaths (vs. 16). To be sure,
these people thought they had some reason for their conduct in Paul's
teachings emphasizing the Christian's freedom. (Paul and his associates had preached in parts of this territory, and his letter to the
Galatians probably circulated among them.) Had Paul not said, "It is
for freedom that Christ has set us free. Stand firm, then, and do not

let yourselves be burdened again by a yoke of slavery" (Gal. 5:1; compare 2:4)? Unfortunately, they did not read on to Galatians 5:13: "You, my brothers, were called to be free. But do not use your freedom to indulge the sinful nature; rather serve one another in love." Slaves were particularly interested in thoughts such as those Paul had written in 1 Corinthians 7:22: "He who was a slave when he was called by the Lord is the Lord's freedman." Women and slaves were stirred by Galatians 3:28: "There is neither Jew nor Greek, slave nor free, male nor female." These were words easy to misunderstand if one were inclined to misunderstand them. So Peter warns his readers to use their freedom responsibly and "live as servants of God" (vs. 16), as indeed Paul had also clearly said.

But perhaps the misunderstandings were not totally wrong, after all. In the gospel were the seeds of a revolution that, in fact, did undermine the rigid social hierarchy with its concern for ranking and honor. Jesus Himself had said, "The greatest among you will be your servant. For whoever exalts himself will be humbled, and whoever humbles himself will be exalted" (Matt. 23:11, 12). It so happened that in the church, a slave might be ordained an elder having spiritual authority over his own master, if the latter was a church member. Such may have been the case with Onesimus, if the overseer of the church in Ephesus at the beginning of the second century (Ignatius, *Ephesians*, 1:3; 6:2) was the same man as the one about whom Paul wrote to Philemon (Philemon 10; compare vs. 16). Though the apostles did not directly attack the institution of slavery, by making all believers brothers and sisters, they certainly sabotaged it.

The punctuation of the NIV in 1 Peter 2:17 makes it appear that the first imperative, "Show proper respect to everyone," meaning "to all human beings, whether believers or unbelievers," is a summary of the next three imperatives, but that is not necessarily correct. It is a series of four commands that sum up what was said beginning at verse 13. The first two commands regard groups, and the second two are about individuals. The same Greek verb is used in the first and fourth command and means "honor" or "respect." Everyone and the emperor (compare Mark 12:17) are to be respected, but different verbs are used for the two middle commands: "Love the brotherhood," in harmony with what Peter had said earlier (1:22), and "Fear God," meaning a reverence that goes beyond anything rendered to the emperor, though Peter may very well be thinking of Proverbs 24:21: "Fear the Lord and the king, my son, and do not join with the rebellious."

So we see that the first thing Peter insists on is good citizenship (using the term loosely or locally, since the majority of his readers were technically not Roman citizens, a privilege granted only to few at that time), though he wanted to remind them that their ultimate loyalty was to God. Paul had insisted on the same thing for similar reasons in Romans 13:1-7. The apostles supported law and order.

Counsel to Slaves

The word used for slaves in 2:18 (*oiketai*) is different from the more usual word (*douloi*) and means household slaves.

The ancient economy and society were heavily dependent on slave labor. (In the Roman Empire, small farmers could not compete with the cheap labor of the ever-increasing number of slaves, so they sold their land to large estates and headed into the cities, where they formed a restless, landless class living on the public dole and clamoring for bread and circuses.) Perhaps one-half of the population was slave. The Greeks and Romans saw nothing wrong in that—it was more humane than killing their captives! One could also be born to a slave mother or go into slavery because of debt. Some even sold themselves into slavery; it guaranteed a certain kind of security—a place to sleep and something to eat. Some slaves actually feared freedom because of the insecurity and hardship it would bring.

Legally, a slave was a thing, not a person, and completely under the power of his master. But he would usually be cared for at least as well as a domestic animal. With some masters, that was not saying very much! The master could inflict cruel punishment. He could torture a slave or cut out his tongue. If the treatment disabled the slave so as to make him useless, he might as well be killed, and often was. Young female slaves had to do their masters' bidding, whatever that was. Young male slaves provided much of the entertainment in the gladiatorial combats of the amphitheaters. But about the time

Peter was writing, the emperors were issuing regulations to restrain excessive cruelty and abuse of slaves.

There were also kind and benevolent masters who treated their slaves well and often set them free, within the limits set by law. And the way was also open for a slave to accumulate a little money and eventually buy his own freedom. A well-educated and skillful slave was usually treated like a member of the family. A slave's identity and pride were bound up with the prestige and honor of his owner, even more so than a person today may draw his sense of identity from the company or organization he works for.

The demographic facts were such that a large proportion of the believers were slaves, and the majority of them belonged to non-Christian masters and mistresses. Their new Christian faith had awakened in them a sense of self-worth and freedom. They really belonged to God, the supreme Owner! They refused to participate in their owners' pagan worship. They could easily give the impression that they were "uppity." Some did not know the difference between liberty and license.

Peter tells the Christian slaves to submit respectfully to their human masters, whether they are kind or cruel (vs. 18). What if you get a beating that you do not deserve? It is far better than getting a beating that you do deserve! You cannot get credit for that, but if you endure a beating for God's sake, He will commend you (vss. 19, 20). Peter's admonition was in harmony with the Sermon on the Mount: "If you love those who love you, what reward will you get?" (Matt. 5:46).

Interpreters debate the meaning of the phrase translated "because he is conscious of God" in 2:19. It could also be translated "because of the conscience of God," perhaps meaning the conscience that God prompts. And what is "commendable"—the mere fact that the slave endures unjust punishment, or the reason why the owner inflicted it? It could mean that because the slave was obedient to the true God, he did not join in his owner's pagan worship, and that was the reason for his punishment. But the main idea seems to be that meekly and resolutely suffering for doing good is the thing that God commends (vs. 20).

That must have been a hard saying in the ears of those poor people, but Peter drives it home profoundly by reminding them that it is no more than what Christ had done for them (vss. 21-25). Movingly, he appeals to a motive that is distinctively Christian—in fact, quintessentially Christian: the imitation of Christ. Peter bases this beautiful passage upon what his readers knew of Christ's trial and execution and upon Isaiah 53, a prophecy that Christians applied from the beginning to Christ's Passion.

The words are strong. "Christ suffered *for you*" (2:21, emphasis supplied), dying in your place. At the same time, He left you *an example*. Here, Peter uses the Greek word *hypogrammos*, a word from the schoolroom. When schoolboys were learning to form letters correctly, they were given a pattern to trace and copy; that was called a *hypogrammos*. Christ left us this pattern to follow, "that you should follow in his steps." In this one verse (vs. 21), all the key doctrines of Christ are included in compressed form: Christ as Saviour and Christ as Example.

Some Christians have seen Christ only as Saviour, suffering vicariously in our stead. Others have seen Him only as an Example, showing us how we must live to be saved. This "either/or" approach leads to a theological dilemma.

How can you have a Jesus human enough to be accessible for imitation, yet divine enough to have power to save? If you make Him too big, how can I be like Him? If you make Him too small, how can He save me? In order for me to be like Him, must you not make Him just like me?

The problem is greater for some contemporary piety than it was for Peter and the other apostles. Though the idea of imitating Christ is most fully developed in 1 Peter, it is found in a few other places of the New Testament: Philippians 2:5-8; 1 Thessalonians 1:6; 2 Thessalonians 3:5; Hebrews 13:13; Mark 8:34 and parallels; John 13:14, 15; Ephesians 5:2; 1 John 2:5b, 6; 1 Corinthians 11:1. If you take the trouble to look up these references, you will see that they virtually all have to do with perseverance in loving self-sacrifice, and suffering, just as in 1 Peter. We simply cannot be like Jesus in every respect—an unmarried Jewish male, an itinerant rabbi with minimal family responsibilities, and in a unique sense, the Son of God. But we are called to imitate Him in willingness to suffer, to take up our cross, to serve rather than to be served, to give our lives if need be. That is the biblical doctrine of imitating Christ. But we can suffer for Him only because He first suffered for us. The imitation of Christ is made possible only by the atonement of Christ. So Peter tells us in 2:24. As Marshall (91) says, "Christ cannot be an example of suffering for us to follow unless he is first of all the Savior whose sufferings were endured on our behalf." Redemption comes first (vs. 25). A. J. Gordon once said: "The imitation of Christ is utterly impossible, apart from incorporation into Christ. . . . It is only the Christ within who can reproduce the Christ without."

Just as Christ, though guiltless, endured abuse and an undeserved death, so must slaves be willing to suffer innocently without resistance or retaliation. Thus they follow in His footsteps, breaking the vicious cycle of retaliation, depending on God for vindication (vss. 22, 23). In Christ, our wanderings have an end (vs. 25).

Counsel to Wives

With wives, says Peter, it is the same (3:1). Submit to your husbands. It is clear that Peter has unbelieving husbands in mind, for they need to be won. Then, even more than now, Christian congregations included a large proportion of women who had unbelieving husbands. The basic principle is stated in 3:1, 2. Try to win your husbands by your behavior, not by words. It is not difficult to imagine that some Christian women, fresh in the enthusiasm of their new faith, had been badgering their husbands to follow them to baptism; or perhaps, flushed with a sense of their Christian liberty and the conviction that in Christ there is neither male nor female, bond nor free, they had become an alarming nuisance at home!

As we have seen, according to Greco-Roman political theory, domestic order was essential to political order. Rebellion at home would lead to rebellion in the streets. Insubordination of wives or children was therefore a serious matter. Also, the Romans were nervous about the new cults that were moving into the empire, and these cults were especially popular with women. Furthermore, Greeks and Romans believed that part of a woman's submission to her father or husband included adherence to his religion. Finally, women were not supposed to dress, talk, or conduct themselves so as to irritate their husbands. If women subordinate themselves to their husbands, said Plutarch,

> they are commended, but if they want to have control, they cut a sorrier figure than the subjects of their control. And control ought to be exercised by the man over the woman, not as the owner has control of a piece of property, but, as the soul controls the body, by entering into her feelings and being knit to her through goodwill (Plutarch, *Advice to Bride and Groom*, 142E [33]).

This is a point upon which Christianity suffered some scandal. The popular idea was that Christianity made a wife hard to live with. This common view is reflected in the famous Roman novel by Apuleius, *The Golden Ass* (9.14). Here, he apparently describes a Christian woman:

> The baker which bought me was an honest and sober man, but his wife the most pestilent woman in all the world, insomuch that he endured with her many miseries and afflictions to his bed and house, so that I myself did secretly pity his estate and bewail his evil fortune: for there was not one single fault that was lacking in her, but all the mischiefs that could be devised had flowed into her heart as into some filthy privy: she was crabbed, cruel, drunken, obstinate, niggish, covetous in base robberies, riotous in filthy expenses, an enemy to faith and chastity, a despiser of all the gods to whom others did honor, one that affirmed that she had instead of our sure religion an only god by herself, whereby inventing empty rites and ceremonies, she deceived all men, but especially her poor husband, delighting in drinking wine, yes early in the morning, and abandoning her body to continual whoredom.

The description is surely libelous, but it illustrates the pagan perception. So a woman's forsaking the religion of her husband and taking up an Eastern cult such as Christianity was regarded as insubordination, and religious insubordination called forth slanders about social insubordination. Peter wants to exhort wives to submissive behavior because he wants to encourage conduct that would contradict the Roman misperceptions and slanders.

After the basic exhortation, Peter gives some counsel on adornment (3:3, 4). A woman's true beauty comes not so much as something outward as something inward. As examples of outward adornment, Peter mentions fancy hairdos, gold jewelry, and fine clothes. It is important to note that Peter is not laying down a distinctively Christian standard. Remember that he is talking about how to win over a pagan husband. Greek men wanted their wives to be submissive, gentle, and quiet. Peter says: Very well, act that way. That is doing good. Disprove the nasty slanders. Do not be like the women of the Isis cult, who were noted for their extravagant apparel and cosmetic display and their rumored immoral conduct.

What Peter was saying about women's adornment was not different from what pagan and Jewish moralists were saying. For example, Phintys (*On the Temperance of a Woman*, 153.15-28) said that a woman's garments should be white and simple; she should not decorate herself with gold and emeralds, for they are very expensive and exhibit pride and arrogance. She should adorn herself with modesty rather than with decoration (summarized in Balch, 101). Musonius, who advocated a mild kind of women's liberation, nevertheless wrote:

> In the first place, a woman must be a good housekeeper. . . . But above all a woman must be chaste and self-controlled; she must, I mean, be pure in respect of unlawful love, exercise restraint in other pleasures, not be a slave to desire, not be contentious, not lavish in expense, not extravagant in dress (Musonius, *That Women Should Study Philosophy*, 10.2-4, 11-14).

Iamblichus reported a speech that the philosopher Pythagoras made to the women of Kroton, in which he said:

> "It is right not to oppose your husband, or else to count it as your victory when he has got his way." . . . He also urged them to say little, and that good, all their lives, and see that what others could say of them was good. . . . Tradition says that his praise of piety caused so great a change in them, in favor of simplicity of dress, that not one of them ventured to wear her expensive clothes, and they dedicated all these—thousands of them—in the temple of Hera (Iamblichus, *On the Pythagorean Life*, 54-56).

(More references can be found in Balch, 115, and Michaels, 159.)

In 3:5, 6 Peter illustrates the kind of conduct he has in mind by referring to "the holy women of the past," probably meaning the wives of the patriarchs: Sarah, Rebecca, Rachel, and Leah (Michaels, 164). He specifically mentions Sarah, whom he holds up as an example to follow, because she "obeyed Abraham and called him her master." In Genesis 18:12 Sarah said, "After I am worn out and my master is old, will I now have this pleasure?" The ancient rabbis noticed that when the Lord repeated to Abraham what Sarah said, in the next verse, He changed her words to "Will I really have a child, now that I am old?" One rabbi suggested that the Lord did this to keep peace in the family! Indeed, what Sarah really said was unflattering to Abraham, but Peter picks out the word *master* (literally, "lord") and uses it to prove that Sarah respected her husband and furnishes a model of obedience and submission. Gentile converts are children of Sarah, says Peter (3:6), if they do as she did. The Bible bases true pedigree on imitation (John 8:39).

The women are to "do what is right" and "not give way to fear" (3:6). A woman's doing right would include refusing to participate in her husband's pagan religion, the only exception to her submission. Even if she deferred to her husband's wishes in every other respect, there was the possibility that her religious orientation might anger him. Even so, says Peter, "Do not give way to fear" (vs. 14).

Counsel to Husbands

The exhortation to husbands (3:7) is much shorter, little more than a footnote. There were probably fewer men in the church than women, but the real reason for the shortness here is probably that this counsel is not concerned with suffering, the theme, and concern of the rest of this domestic code.

Husbands are not told to submit to their wives; the words "in the same way" simply connect this counsel to the preceding series. Peter tells husbands to live considerately with their wives, which may mean sensitivity in sexual relations. But what the Greek literally says is, "Cohabit according to knowledge," and includes all aspects of marriage. Michaels (154, 167) translates: "You husbands in turn must know how to live with a woman." They are to show respect to womankind as the weaker vessel (so says the Greek literally), "vessel" probably meaning body (2 Cor. 4:7), but above all, because the two of them are coheirs of the grace of life. The word *life* refers to the eternal life that husband and wife will both enjoy with God at the end of history. With these words, Peter acknowledges that on the spiritual level, the sexes are equal (Gal. 3:28).

Peter adds yet another reason for treating wives kindly: "So that nothing will hinder your prayers." Our horizontal relationships with other people affect our vertical relationship with God (Matt. 5:23, 24). When husband and wife do not treat each other as coheirs and do not agree in their prayers (Matt. 18:19), it is hard for them to pray and hard for God to answer.

General Counsels

In 3:8-12 Peter sums up the general principles that should apply in all relationships—in the family, in the church, in our relationships with the general society.

In 3:8 he lists five qualities that should characterize Christians in their relationships—particularly in relationships with believers (note the reference to brotherly love). Christians are to be in harmony, sympathetic, having brotherly love, compassionate, and humble.

These qualities are not distinct from each other but rather reinforce each other. Peter may be acquainted with Paul's letter to the Romans (Peter was writing from Rome), for this list of virtues and the admonitions in the next verse summarize Romans 12:14-17.

The harmony (literally "like-minded") that the apostles wanted was not an imposed uniformity of opinion (Rom. 14), but an absence of divisions caused by doctrinal disputes or personal rivalries (1 Cor. 1:10-12).

To be sympathetic means sharing the feelings of others—rejoicing with those who rejoice and mourning with those who mourn (Rom. 12:15). This requires time, sensitivity, and vulnerability—commodities that are rare in the modern world. Perhaps we are reluctant to open ourselves up to the pain of others because we fear that we cannot do anything to help. We need to know that just lending a listening ear helps.

Brotherly love is special consideration that we have for fellow Christians. As we saw in 1:22, this virtue is especially crucial because if church relationships go sour, the strife is especially bitter.

Compassionate means "tenderhearted." The Greek means literally "having good guts," pointing up the psychosomatic nature of feelings. (In English we use the expressions "a pain in the neck" and "my gut reaction.")

Being humble was a specifically Christian virtue; pagans did not particularly cultivate it. It is hard to be humble, because the moment we think we are humble, we no longer are; some people are very proud of their humility! Besides, it is easy to confuse genuine humility with certain pathological states of mind, such as a poor self-image, an inferiority complex, or self-hatred. In fact, arrogance is often just a coverup for such insecure feelings.

In 3:9 the admonition deals especially with how to relate to unbelievers who abuse us, but it could also apply to some situations in the church! Return good for evil. That advice, of course, is taken from the Sermon on the Mount (Matt. 5:38-48; Luke 6:27, 28). "To this you were called" parallels 2:21. Jesus calls us to imitate Him in doing good to those who do us ill. Just as the slaves who do so will receive God's commendation, so will those who follow the counsel here inherit the blessing that Jesus promised in Matthew 5:5, 11, 12.

Peter clinches this point by quoting Psalm 34:12-16, the same psalm he alluded to in 2:3. The evil that the psalm mentions at the end of Peter's quotation (3:12, "the face of the Lord is against those who do evil") must here mean for Peter retaliation against the unbelievers who have been abusing believers because of their religion.

■ Getting Into the Word

1 Peter 3:13–4:11

Again read the whole section, beginning with 2:11, to see how this part is related to the earlier part. Then do a concentrated reading of 3:13 to 4:11, as usual trying to understand why Peter wants to say these things. Now see what you can discover about the following points.

1. How is this section related to the preceding one? Notice what things are repeated that have been introduced before. Why does Peter repeat these things? What is new in this section?
2. List all the things that Peter says about Christ in this section. What would we know about Christ if we had only the information in this section?
3. What does Peter say about baptism? What does that have to do with Noah? What does it have to do with Christ?
4. Is 3:17 related to what goes before or to what comes next or to both? In what way?
5. Where before has Peter talked about the dissipated pagan lifestyle that he describes in 4:3, 4?
6. What is the relation of 4:6 to 3:18, 19?
7. What does Peter say about prayer in 4:7? Do you see any relation to what he said in 3:7?
8. What scripture does Peter allude to in 4:8? Is that scripture used anywhere else in the New Testament? The marginal notes in your Bible should tell you. Are all three places making the same point?

9. **What does Peter say about spiritual gifts? Which ones does he specifically mention? Using your marginal references or a concordance, find the other places in the New Testament where spiritual gifts are mentioned. List all the gifts mentioned. (Someone has counted nineteen different ones.) Do you think this is a complete list of all the gifts that the Spirit gives?**

10. **Compare 1 Peter 3:14b, 15a with Isaiah 8:12, 13. What has Peter done with Isaiah?**

■ Exploring the Word

Dealing With Slander and Hostility

Our impression that the trials and persecution these Christians were facing were not general and official, but rather unplanned harassment and slander and family problems, is borne out by the next five verses (3:13-17), which tell the right way to react to abuse. They assume that suffering is not inevitable if the readers do right. They may escape serious trouble if they conform to the best moral standards of society and prove that Christians are not bad people. But they must continue to reverence Christ as Lord and be ready to give an answer when their faith is challenged. Their irreproachable behavior will provide a platform for them to do that. (Such advice would not have saved anyone during the persecutions at the end of the century and later, when it was a crime just to be a Christian.)

If Christians suffer in spite of doing good, however, they are blessed. Peter has said all this before (2:12-20). In fact, he repeats several things he has said before. Doing good (3:13) was introduced in 2:14. The warning against doing evil (3:17) was anticipated in 3:12. Suffering (3:14, 17) as a theme appeared in 1:6, 11 and in the counsel to slaves (2:19, 21, 23), and he will talk about it again later. Slander and malicious talk (3:16) was also a concern in 2:12. The idea of suffering unjustly (3:14) surfaced in 2:19. And doing God's will (3:17) came up in 2:15. All of this shows how closely the present passage is related to what came before (see Balch, 125, 126). It also shows what Peter's main concerns are.

Peter concedes that refraining from doing wrong is not insurance against trouble. Suffering in spite of doing good is a possibility (though Peter regarded it as a remote possibility, according to the form of the Greek verb). But here is the attitude his readers should have in such an experience: Even if you suffer, not just in spite of doing good, but because of doing good, you will have God's blessing (3:14). At this point Peter quotes Isaiah 8:12 ("Do not be frightened") and goes on to give a Christian paraphrase or explanation of Isaiah 8:13. Isaiah had written, "The Lord Almighty is the one you are to regard as holy"; Peter puts it down as "But in your hearts set apart Christ as Lord." Peter clearly regarded Jesus of Nazareth as the Lord God. Peter is also saying the same thing he told the Sanhedrin in Acts 5:29: Fear and obey God rather than man (compare Matt. 10:28).

Peter now tells his readers to be always prepared to give a reply to everyone who demands a reason for their hope (3:15b). When Christians departed from the traditional customs and changed their lifestyles for religious reasons, they had to face hostile or curious questions, and then they must be able to defend their conduct verbally, as Paul did before Agrippa in Acts 26. But just as Paul did, they should do so courteously (3:16a). The "hope" that is in them (3:15b) is the same living hope Peter spoke about in 1:3, a distinctive possession of Christians. A clear "conscience" (3:16) is something Peter spoke about in 2:19, making a similar point, and in 3:21 he will tell how to get such a conscience. A clear conscience means awareness of God and personal integrity before God (Michaels, 190). If we do not have that, our words of witness will have no power. Our walk must match our talk!

There are three kinds of suffering: the kind that all people experience (pain, sickness, death), the kind that comes because we do wrong (merited punishment), and Christian suffering, which comes because of obeying God in this world. The last kind is a blessed privilege because we share in Christ's suffering. If we suffer, not because of evil that we do, but because of what we are, then our suffering brings honor to what we are and whom we represent. A religion can be discredited by apostates but never by martyrs.

Victory Through Suffering

Peter has said that it is a blessing to suffer for doing right, not fearing hostile people (3:14, 17), and to defend the Christian way, keeping a good conscience (vss. 15, 16). Now he will supply a theological reason, which he introduces with the word *for* (or "because," vs. 18). The first part of 3:18 is clear enough: Christ died for sins once for all (compare Rom. 6:10) to bring us to God. This means that His death was a supreme sacrifice that will not be repeated, that pays our penalty and sets us free from the sin that separated us from God. As Ellen White wrote,

> Christ was treated as we deserve, that we might be treated as He deserves. He was condemned for our sins, in which He had no share, that we might be justified by His righteousness, in which we had no share. He suffered the death which was ours, that we might receive the life which was His. "With His stripes we are healed" (White, *The Desire of Ages*, 25).

Unfortunately, the rest of what Peter wrote from here on to 4:6 is not so easy to grasp. He has crammed together a number of ideas that are older than this letter. This passage has been called one of the most difficult in the entire Bible (Vaughan and Lea, 89).

There are at least four different interpretations of 3:18b-22, and commentators generally list three of them. Then they go on to defend their choice, usually disclaiming dogmatism. Even Adventist interpreters do not agree. At the end of 3:18, George Rice (95) defends the KJV and NIV rendering "by the Spirit," understanding the words to refer to power of the Holy Spirit. The *Seventh-day Adventist Bible Commentary* (7:574) holds that the phrase should be translated "in spirit," referring to Christ's divine existence, in contrast to His earthly existence as a human being. (It could also be interpreted in the light of 1 Corinthians 15:44.) Both interpretations can find support. The discussions of this whole passage can be long and technical, and those who wish to know the details should con-

sult the references given at the end of this chapter. But it is only fair
to explain briefly what the options are, attempt a few conclusions,
and indicate what Peter's main point is.

1. One old interpretation of 3:18b-20 is that Christ in person during the three days between His death and resurrection went to hell
and preached to the spirits of the sinners who had died at the time of
Noah's flood, perhaps to give them a second chance. Besides run-
ning contrary to several basic teachings of the Bible, this interpretation clashes with what the rest of the passage says. Note that 3:18b
indicates that whatever Christ did, He did it *after* He was "made
alive" (resurrected).

2. A view advocated by most Adventist commentators and many
others is that Christ before His incarnation by the Holy Spirit
preached on earth through the instrumentality of Noah to the antediluvian sinners while they were still alive. This position holds that
"in prison" refers figuratively to their spiritual condition. But why
would Peter call live men and women "spirits," since he does not so
refer to the eight who were saved?

3. Another view is that the "spirits in prison" were the sinners to
whom Peter and the other apostles preached as instruments of Christ,
and that Noah and the antediluvians are brought in for comparison.
In order to make this view work, commentators have to ignore the
plain meaning of words and assume that a clause is left out or implied. Very few commentators see any light in this interpretation.

4. Some variation of a fourth view is held by a large majority of
modern scholars. According to this interpretation, Christ proclaimed
His victory to the fallen angels (compare 2 Pet. 2:4; Jude 6) after His
resurrection but before His final ascent to heaven. Angels are called
"spirits" (Heb. 1:14; Acts 23:8, 9), and so are evil beings (Mark 1:23;
Luke 10:20; Acts 19:15, 16). The Greek word translated "preach"
here is not the same word as "evangelize," though it can sometimes
mean that. It can also simply mean to make a proclamation, as in
Revelation 5:2.

Scholars point out that in the first century, many stories circulated
about Enoch (Gen. 5:24), who could travel around the heavens and
even act as a messenger to the angels who fell before the Flood. Many

of these legends are found in two books, one of which is now part of the Ethiopian Coptic Bible and has been found among the Dead Sea Scrolls. This book is known as 1 Enoch or Ethiopic Enoch. In 1 Enoch 12:4 Enoch is sent to the fallen angels to tell them they have no hope:

> Behold, the Watchers called to me, Enoch the scribe, and said to me, Enoch, scribe of righteousness, go, inform the Watchers of heaven who have left the high heaven and the holy eternal place, and have corrupted themselves with the women, and have done as the sons of men do, and have taken wives for themselves, and have become completely corrupt on the earth. They will have on earth neither peace nor forgiveness of sin.

(See also 1 Enoch 10:1-15, which speaks of the Flood and of the casting of the fallen angels into the prison of the abyss and destruction in the lake of fire.)

It has been pointed out that these and other stories about Enoch are somewhat parallel to what Peter says about Christ, as though Enoch is a type and Christ the antitype, and Peter draws imagery from the Enoch legend to dramatize Christ's victory over the powers of evil (Marshall, 129). Marshall goes on to speculate:

> This way of presenting things may have come to Peter either by direct revelation or by meditation on the available scriptural and extracanonical materials. Either way, of course, the Spirit of God was active in the process, whether granting direct knowledge or working concursively with Peter's mental processes (ibid.).

However all that may be, the interpretation that the spirits in prison are fallen angels accords with 3:22, for "authorities and powers" can also refer to the fallen angels. Colossians 2:15 speaks of the same victory: "Having disarmed the powers and authorities, he made a public spectacle of them, triumphing over them by the cross."

Peter's point in all this is that after death comes resurrection and victory. Christ's victory assures that of His followers, for His victory is theirs. He conquered death and the hostile powers arrayed against Him, and so will His followers. For behind the earthly powers that harass and persecute believers are malignant spiritual powers. But fear not; they are defeated.

That is the theological basis of their confidence, but Peter is not finished yet. He sees baptism as an antitype of the water of the Flood (3:21). Just as only the eight persons who entered the ark found salvation, so only those who accept baptism and all that it signifies will be saved. (The parallel is a little bent, since water was a threat to Noah, but it brought salvation to Christians. Of course, the analogy was not meant to walk on all fours.) Peter insists, however, that we are not to think of baptism in a magical or physical sense. The spiritual experience it signifies is what counts. It is "the pledge of a good conscience toward God." In Greek "good conscience" is exactly the same expression Peter used in 3:16, making an important connection. Peter goes on to say that it is really the resurrection of Jesus Christ that makes baptism effective. So the mere physical act of baptism is nothing by itself. Two things give it efficacy: objectively, what Christ has done; and subjectively, the candidate's disposition of heart and intention of mind.

Jesus is "at God's right hand" (3:22). In the ancient Mediterranean world, the position at the right hand of a king was the place of honor. Colossians 3:1 says Christ is "seated" there. In Stephen's vision of Acts 7:55, 56 he saw Christ "standing" there. There is something metaphorical about all visions of heaven (compare John 3:12, 13).

The whole passage of 3:18 to 4:6 is divided into two parts: declaration and exhortation. The theme that runs through it is the contrast between flesh and spirit. Section 4:1-6 is an exhortation to baptized believers to abstain from evil, for they are spiritually liberated through suffering. Verse 4:1a links back to 3:18a, declaring that Christ died/suffered in the body. When Christians "arm [themselves] with the same attitude" they prepare for persecution, because ("therefore") they know that His suffering led to victory.

The rest of 4:1 is a little difficult. Who is the "he" in the statement, "He who has suffered in his body is done with sin"? If it is the Christian, how does suffering make him cease from sin? If it is Christ, in what sense did He cease from sin, since that implies that He was sinning before He ceased from it? The preceding context favors the interpretation that "he who has suffered" is Christ, the one who suffered in 3:18. Christ did not sin and then stop sinning because He suffered, but "he has finished dealing with it [on the cross], once and for all; he has put it behind him, says Peter, and so should we" (Michaels, 228). So the Christian is in the picture also, because he identifies with Christ. So the "he" in 4:2 is the Christian, who now lives the rest of his life for God.

Verse 3 shows that the readers were former pagans. Peter lists their former vices, which are like the works of the flesh listed in Galatians 5:19-21 and Romans 13:13. He mentions three kinds of sins: sexual, alcoholic, and idolatrous. We have seen how licentiousness was a feature of the popular culture. It was also a feature of many religious festivals, such as the Saturnalia (celebrated on December 25). That is why Peter associates immorality with idolatry. In Romans 1:18-32 Paul identified idolatry as the origin and root of such evils.

Peter acknowledges that their former friends do not take kindly to it when Christians forsake their revels (4:4). The local bar is a sort of church, and its members do not like it when one of them joins another denomination! But the abusive carousers will soon have to give an account to the Judge (vs. 5).

The statement in 4:6 has caused difficulty because it has wrongly been interpreted in conjunction with 3:18-22. It must be dealt with differently. The Greek verb is different, this time meaning "evangelize." The NIV has probably given the right meaning: "The gospel was preached even to those who are now dead" but before they died. They were Christian converts who died after hearing the gospel. It is intended as an explanation of the last part of the preceding verse: God is "ready to judge the living and the dead." Peter wants to contrast the fate of the abusive unbelievers with that of the abused believers. The pagans were passing judgment on the Christians, but they shall be judged by God. The Christians may be judged by the pagans in the body, but in the resurrection ("in the spirit") they will have eternal life. "Being alive in the spirit" is what Paul calls being "changed" in 1 Corinthians 15:51, 52.

Preparing for the End

The mention of the judgment and the resurrection leads to the next subject. Peter believed that the end of all things was near (4:7). In view of that, he lays down a few short commands that deal mostly with church life. In the New Testament, mention of the nearness of the second advent is always linked to a demand for repentance and godly conduct. Belief in Christ's soon coming is worthless if it does not affect the way we live.

The first is counsel regarding prayer. Peter recognizes that there are hindrances to prayer. One is marital discord (3:8). Another is doing evil (vs. 12). Here, he says that Christians must be "clear minded and self-controlled." They must be mentally alert and sensible, as he has already said in 1:13. The preparation for the advent is not faddish excitement but quiet prayerfulness. Fanaticism is not the way to stay the course.

Next, he tells his readers again and "above all" to love each other to the maximum that they can make their love stretch and says "love covers over a multitude of sins" (4:8). This may be a reference to Proverbs 10:12, a verse also quoted at the end of James (5:20). Whose sins are covered? Does this mean that if we love someone, if we overlook his or her faults, or that if we love, our own sins are covered by God? The verse in Proverbs suggests the former, meaning that I do not hold a grudge because of an offense that someone has committed against me. Christians need to cultivate the ability to ask for and to grant forgiveness sincerely. If they do not, when times of trouble come, the enemy will easily exploit their mutual antagonisms.

One practical way of showing love to fellow believers is to offer hospitality without complaining (4:9). Hospitality was an important virtue, because in those days there were no decent hotels or motels. Inns generally had a very bad atmosphere; they were places of wine, prostitutes, and crime. But in the early church there was much movement and travel, as can be seen in Paul's letters and the book of Acts. So Christians gave lodging, even room and board, to Christian visitors. But apparently some people complained that they had too many visitors. Perhaps some visitors even abused the hospitality. An early church manual, called the *Didache* (11:2, 3), says that if a visiting apostle or prophet stays longer than a couple of days, he is a false prophet! But Peter says to practice hospitality without complaining.

The next two verses (4:10, 11) speak of spiritual gifts, perhaps triggered by the thought that hospitality is a gift. Once again, Peter shows that he is familiar with Romans 12, for he here summarizes Romans 12:6-8, though he gives it his own emphasis and mentions only two specific examples. He indicates that each Christian has received at least one gift (compare 1 Cor. 12:7), of which he is a steward, and he or she must use it to serve one another. A steward (*oikonomos*) was a person, often a slave, who had the responsibility of managing a man's estate, giving out food to workers, paying wages, and other such duties. But none of the things he handled were the property of the steward. Each Christian is thus, in his or her own way, a channel of the very grace of God. God speaks through him or her, and the service is performed in God's strength, so the praise for these things belongs to God.

The New Testament contains several lists of spiritual gifts, none of them exactly the same as another. Probably a complete list would have hundreds of gifts. The list in Romans 12:6-8 begins with the two examples that Peter mentions. When Peter reflects that the power in all spiritual gifts comes from God and that the ultimate purpose is "that in all things God may be praised," he breaks out into a doxology and closes this section with a great "Amen."

■ Applying the Word

1 Peter 2:11–4:11

1. **How can I be in the world but not of the world? How does being a Christian affect my citizenship?**
2. **In the country where I live, does a concern for "family values" and social stability threaten religious liberty?**

3. The society in which Peter worked had a culture of submission and hierarchy, while in America and Western countries, we promote a culture of liberty and equality. How does that affect the way I apply Peter's counsels today?

4. What is my reputation where I work and live, and what reputation do I give to my church?

5. As a Christian, what special reasons do I have for obeying secular laws?

6. How can I show respect to people in authority? Should I do it?

7. If Peter had been writing a generation later, in the time of John the revelator, would he have had the same attitude toward the government? How would I apply his counsels if I were living under a government like that of Hitler, Stalin, Idi Amin, Pol Pot, or Saddam Hussein?

8. How do I relate to my employer or employees? What difference does being a Christian make? When I am mistreated, should I always "turn the other cheek"?

9. What difference does being a Christian make in the way I relate to my spouse?

10. In what ways can I imitate Christ? In what ways can I not?

11. Is social and moral disintegration in my society related to a loss of respect for authority, and does it point to a need for authoritarianism? Why, or why not?

12. Society's expectations for women and wives have changed a great deal since Peter's time. How does that affect the way we should apply his counsels?

13. Is there a permanent principle involved in Peter's and Paul's admonitions regarding dress, jewelry, and hairstyles? If so, how do I apply it today?

14. How can Christian women (or men) win over an unbelieving spouse? When are words appropriate, and when inappropriate? Was Peter inconsistent when he insisted on speaking about the gospel in Acts 4:18-20, but advised wives not to do so in 1 Peter 3:1?

15. Would my marriage be any different if I always thought of

my spouse as a coheir of eternal life?

16. Is it possible for my prayers and those of my spouse to be opposite? If so, how can God answer them?

17. How does my behavior toward church members compare to the way I treat nonmembers?

18. Have I ever suffered for doing the right thing? Would I have done it anyway? Are there situations in which I fear to do the Christian thing? Why?

19. Can I defend my faith? Does my walk match my talk?

20. How do I relate to Christ—as my Saviour or as my Example? How can He be both? How are these two things related?

21. How should I feel about evil spirits?

22. What did my baptism do for me?

23. What are my feelings about the judgment day?

24. Do I hold a grudge against a fellow church member? What should I do about it?

25. In what ways do we still need to show hospitality? Why?

26. What spiritual gift or gifts do I have?

∎ Researching the Word

1. Using your concordance, find all the references to "authorities and powers" (in the KJV translated "principalities and powers") or "powers and authorities," and try to decide what each reference is speaking of.

2. Find all the New Testament references to the death of Christ, and write down what each says His death accomplished.

3. Find all the places in the Bible that speak of dress and adornment (e.g., Revelation 21:2). What position does the Bible take about beauty?

∎ Further Study of the Word

1. For an interesting study of social values in Peter's world, such as honor and rank, see B. J. Malina, *The New Testament World: Insights From Cultural Anthropology*. A useful refer-

ence book for such matters is J. J. Pilch and B. J. Malina, *Biblical Social Values and Their Meanings: A Handbook*. Particularly notice the short articles on Dyadism and Honor.

2. On the moral and social conditions of the time, see S. Angus, *The Environment of Early Christianity*, 30-67; also F. Lyall, *Slaves, Citizens, Sons: Legal Metaphors in the Epistles*, 27-46. See also the article by B. Witherington, "Why Not Idol Meat?" in *Bible Review*, June 1994, 38-43, 54.

3. The best study of the domestic codes is D. L. Balch, *Let Wives Be Submissive: The Domestic Code in 1 Peter*. See also Balch's chapter in D. E. Aune, ed., *Greco-Roman Literature and the New Testament: Selected Forms and Genres*, 25-50. Balch is also a rich source for Greco-Roman ideas about the place of wives and other matters referred to in 1 Peter.

4. The basic work setting out the view of the majority of modern scholars regarding "the spirits in prison" is W. J. Dalton, *Christ's Proclamation to the Spirits: A Study of 1 Peter 3:18–4:6*. See also the relevant parts of the commentaries of Selwyn, Kelly, Michaels, and Marshall. For the view that the spirits were living people in the time of Noah, see F. D. Nichol, ed., *Seventh-day Adventist Bible Commentary*, 7:574-576; G. E. Rice, *A Living Hope*, 89-97; C. Vaughan and T. D. Lea, *1, 2 Peter, Jude*, 94-102.

5. Most of the quotations and references from Greek and Roman pagan authors that appeared in this chapter can be found in the appropriate volumes of the Loeb Classical Library. One quotation was from G. Clark, trans., Iamblichus, *On the Pythagorean Life*. The book of 1 Enoch can be found in H. F. D. Sparks, ed., *The Apocryphal Old Testament*, 169-319.

CHAPTER FOUR

Preparing the Church for Crisis

1 Peter 4:12–5:14

Peter has already had Silas write a doxology and an Amen in 4:11, but his heart is still full, and he is not ready to end the letter. Perhaps they had stopped for lunch or had a night's sleep, and now they return to the writing. Remember that they did not write with computers! If the Lord gave Peter some new thoughts on themes he had already dealt with, he can only go on and add them, not revise what he wrote before without starting over and revising his whole letter.

So once again Peter addresses his readers/hearers, "Dear Friends" (literally "Beloved") and has another go at themes he has dealt with before, but with some new urgency and new angles (4:12-19). He wants to emphasize the joy and endurance Christians will need as the trials they will suffer intensify.

In 5:1-11 Peter begins with a sort of domestic code for relationships in the church, how elders and young members should relate to each other. This leads to an exhortation to humility and then to alertness and steadfastness in the face of the devil's attacks. This ends in a promise and a doxology.

Before Peter and Silas fold up the letter to send, Peter adds a personal note and some greetings (5:12-14).

■ Getting Into the Word

1 Peter 4:12-19

Read the passage once from beginning to end. Then read the eight verses again, but begin with verse 19, and read them in reverse order. Did you notice anything you missed before? Now

read the passage in the proper order, this time noticing the con-
junctions (linking words such as *but, for, if, so*) that join each
verse to the one before it, thus determining the relationship
the thoughts have with each other. Now pay attention to the
following points.

1. List all the points you remember that Peter has made before; then go back and find the places where he has said them
   before (usually more than once!). List those places. Now try
   to detect what new twist Peter gives these themes in the
   present passage.
2. Is there any totally new point in the passage? What is it?
3. What scriptures does Peter allude to or quote? Compare their
   original contexts with the way Peter uses them here. (You
   can use your Bible's concordance or marginal notes to perform this operation.)
4. List all the reasons for suffering mentioned in the passage.
5. What two phases of judgment are mentioned?

■ Exploring the Word

Don't Be Surprised by Troubles

Peter begins by telling the believers not to be surprised by the
"fiery trial" that is happening to them (4:12, KJV). The NIV translates it "painful trial," and such suffering is no doubt painful, but this
translation causes us to miss the allusion Peter is making to passages
such as Isaiah 48:10; Malachi 3:2, 3; Psalm 66:10; and Proverbs 27:21,
an allusion he earlier made in 1:7. Just as the metallurgist purifies
and tests metal with fire, the Lord uses fiery trials to refine His people.

Jews were somewhat accustomed to religious persecution, but for
Gentiles this was a new experience, and they were bewildered by it.
Peter wanted to fortify them for the problems they were having in
their families, neighborhoods, and towns.

Why would they be surprised at their troubles? When the worst
happens to us, we seldom expect it. Our cry is, "Why me, Lord?
What have I done to deserve this?" Besides, those poor people had

believed that when they obeyed and followed the Lord, He would bless them. Peter has news for them: Their very suffering is a blessing. That is what he is going to explain in the next few verses.

Peter tells them to rejoice in their trials (4:13). James had said the same thing (James 1:2) but for a different reason. James says it builds character. Peter would not disagree, but he offers a profounder reason: they "participate in the sufferings of Christ." They suffer as He suffered, and He suffered as they suffer. When they think of the cross, they can say: "Half mine!" Of course, their suffering does not contribute to the atonement. Christ's suffering and death were unique in that sense. But their suffering is of a similar kind and for the same reason—the great controversy with evil. Of course, that is not the only reason for rejoicing in their suffering. That alone would be merely exalted masochism. Rather, the end result will be their joy when they see Christ's glorious second coming ("when his glory is revealed"). As they share now Christ's suffering, they will share then His resurrection, vindication, and glory. There is no clearer doctrine in the New Testament than the doctrine of suffering as the prelude to glory (Matt. 5:11, 12; Luke 6:22, 23; Heb. 10:32-39; 11:26; 13:13, 14; Rom. 8:17; 2 Cor. 1:5-7; Phil. 3:10, 11; 2 Tim. 2:11; and many others).

Peter now speaks of the right reason (4:14, 16) and the wrong reason (vs. 15) for suffering. The good reason for enduring abuse is simply because we are Christians. A generation later it was a capital offense just to be a Christian. At the time Peter wrote, it was merely a stigma. If you are reproached and insulted for bearing the name of Christ, says Peter, "you are blessed" (vs.14). Of course, that is what Jesus had said in the Sermon on the Mount (Matt. 5:11, 12). The wrong reason for suffering is that we have actually done wrong (4:15)!

Peter lists four examples of wrongdoing. It is clear enough what a murderer or a thief is, and the third term is generic for any kind of criminal malfeasance. But the fourth category deserves some comment. Peter's Greek word means literally "someone who supervises other people's affairs." Our colloquial term is a "busybody." That is not normally a felony or even a misdemeanor, but Peter adds it to the list, though somewhat set off from the other three things. It was not a crime, but it was something that would bring reproach upon the Christian community, because busybodies were not liked in the Greco-Roman world. Some philosophers had appointed themselves as overseers of private morality, going around from house to house to see who was quarreling, who was making their children behave, who had bad habits, and the like. Epictetus actually tried to defend such moral supervision. But Plutarch wrote an essay on busybodies and said:

> Nowadays there are doormen . . . to give warning, so that the stranger might not catch the mistress of the house or the unmarried daughter unawares, or a slave being punished or the maidservants screaming. But it is for these very things that the busybody slips in (Plutarch, *On Curiosity*, 516DE, quoted in Balch, 93).

Paul warned about being a busybody (2 Thess. 3:11; 1 Tim. 5:13). There have always been Christians who are self-appointed moral watchdogs, sure that they know what is best for other people, always ready with unsolicited advice. Peter is saying that if you suffer for that, you deserve it!

On the other hand, if you suffer for the name of Christ, you have no need to be ashamed, and "the Spirit of glory and of God rests on you" (4:14). Perhaps Peter is remembering what Jesus said:

> When they arrest you, do not worry about what to say or how to say it. At that time you will be given what to say, for it will not be you speaking, but the Spirit of your Father speaking through you (Matt. 10:19, 20).

In 4:17 Peter introduces a new thought, based on Ezekiel 9:6 (compare Mal. 3:1-6). Judgment begins at God's house. The troubles that were beginning were just the opening phase of God's plan for the end. They would purify the church, which is God's temple, by sifting out hypocrites. But what the suffering Christians were enduring was nothing compared to what will happen to those who reject God's message. Christians are suffering oppression now, but soon it will be the oppressors' turn. As is his custom, Peter clinches this point with a scriptural quotation, this time from Proverbs 11:31.

So, concludes Peter, if you are suffering according to God's will, take courage, and hang in there (4:19).

■ Getting Into the Word

1 Peter 5:1-11

Read this passage through once to get the general flow; then read it again carefully, and try writing an outline of it, with main headings and subheadings. Then consider the following questions and issues.

1. What two kinds of church members does Peter address? What specific counsels does he give to each? What motivation does he mention for each?
2. How does this passage resemble a domestic code, especially those earlier in the letter? What is different about this one?
3. For whom are the admonitions in 5:6-9 intended?
4. What scriptural allusions and quotations are in this passage?
5. With the help of a concordance, look up the places in both Testaments where "elders" are mentioned, and try to determine the meaning in each.
6. With a concordance, find all the references you can containing the words *humble* and *humility*. Write down in your notebook the meanings that you find.

■ Exploring the Word

Good Relationships in the Church as the Key to Survival

Peter seems to change the subject abruptly at 5:1. But it is not really unrelated, for what he is about to say is very important for a church that is facing persecution. When feelings between church members are sour, the devil and his servants can exploit the situation with devastating effect.

Peter employs a form rather similar to the domestic code he used earlier, but it is a distinctly Christian domestic code, because no non-Christian code would deal with roles and duties in the church.

Peter begins by addressing the elders (vss. 1-4). An elder, of course, is literally an older person. In ancient society, and still in traditional societies, leadership normally devolved upon older men. When the culture does not change very much or very fast, age and experience are an indispensable advantage for acting as a leader of the community. Consequently, "elder" took on the secondary meaning of "leader." Such was the case in Judaism (e.g., Acts 4:5, 8). This usage was immediately passed on to the early church (e.g., Acts 14:23). In Peter's code here, the group in subordinate relationship to the elders is called "young men" (5:5), but the duties that Peter describes in 5:2-4 suggest that the term here denotes holders of a church office, not primarily an age group. Of course, there was some correspondence between age and responsibility, or the contrast with the young men would not have made sense.

The Greek word for elder is *presbyteros*, from which we get the words *Presbyterian* and *priest*. But the Greek word originally had none of the meanings that the word *priest* acquired. Similarly, the English word *bishop* comes from the Greek word *episkopos* (whence comes also our word *Episcopalian*), which literally means "overseer" or "supervisor." In the earliest Christian church, the titles *presbyteros* and *episkopos* were used interchangeably for the same office, with the first word referring to status and the second to function. For example, Acts 20:17 says that Paul sent for the *presbyteroi* of the church, but in 20:28, Paul addresses these same elders and reminds them that the Holy Spirit has made them *episkopoi* of the flock. We find the same synonymous use in our passage here, for in verse 2, Peter says the elders are serving as overseers (*episkopoi*).

In our passage, Peter makes his appeal to the holders of this office "as a fellow elder," not as a bishop, archbishop, metropolitan, or pope. Those are offices of which the early church knew nothing. Peter does not pull rank on them, though he is an apostle. He appeals to them as a brother.

It is interesting that the churches had these officers who performed pastoral functions, though each member had a spiritual gift (4:10, 11). This circumstance teaches us something about ministry in the apostolic churches. There was a sense in which every member was a minister and expected to perform a ministry. But there were nevertheless people in charge.

Though Peter does not pull rank, he does not hesitate to remind them of his special authority. He was an eyewitness of Christ's sufferings (5:1) and resurrection, as he noted in his pentecostal sermon (Acts 2:32). So when he spoke about "the glory to be revealed" (compare 4:13), he knew what he was talking about.

Peter's charge to these men is that they serve willingly and unselfishly as "shepherds of God's flock" (5:2). Our word *pastor* comes from the Latin word for shepherd. It is not clear whether at that early period there were professional, paid pastors. Money was not to be their motive of service (vs. 2). It is probably true that men who gave their full time to service as shepherds of God's flock were financially compensated, just as an itinerant evangelist like Paul could have been so supported, had he chosen to be (1 Cor. 9:7-12). Paul in 1 Timothy 5:17 instructs: "The elders who direct the affairs of the church well are worthy of double pay [that is the meaning here of the Greek *timē*], especially those whose work is preaching and teaching."

Likewise their motive is not to be love of power and authority; they are to lead by example more than by overbearing command (5:3). That is in harmony with Jesus' teaching in Matthew 23:8-12, Luke 9:46-48, and especially Luke 22:24-27. Paul similarly instructed Titus to lead by example (Titus 2:7).

Peter calls Christ the Chief Shepherd (5:4). In 2:25 he had identified Him as "the Shepherd and Overseer of your souls." When He returns He will bestow the ultimate reward for the faithful service of the undershepherds. The role of shepherd of God's flock must have been especially meaningful to the apostle whom Jesus had personally charged, "Take care of my sheep" (John 21:15-17).

Having made that appeal to the elders, Peter now gives a balancing mandate to the "young men." There has been quite a bit of discussion about the meaning of this term. It seems to mean simply everyone who is not an elder. While the elders are not to lord it over them, they are to submit to the elders. (The NIV, trying to solve the problem of the contrast with "young men," changes the translation of *presbyteroi* here to "those who are older," but there is no warrant for translating the word differently in the two places.) These instructions bespeak an exquisite courtesy: the elders do not heavy-handedly insist on their authority, but the young men defer to their authority. Peter enjoins humility upon the young men (5:5), but in the light of his total counsel, both groups should exemplify humility (compare 3:8). Indeed, he says to show humility "toward one another." Here, Peter again drives his point home with a scriptural quotation, Proverbs 3:34.

The Greek word for *humble* is *tapeinos*. Humility was a virtue among the Jews, and the verse in Proverbs is quite typical. But among the Greek moralists it was considered a vice, while pride was a virtue. For them, it was no compliment to say that a person "has no pride." For example, when Epictetus wanted to describe the kind of person he disliked, the first thing he mentioned was that he was *tapeinos*, followed by "hypercritical, quick-tempered, cowardly, finding fault with everything, blaming everybody, never quiet, a wind-bag"—in other words, a loser (Epictetus, *Discourses*, 3.2.14). But Christianity continued in the Jewish tradition, rather than the Greek. "Blessed are the poor in spirit" (Matt. 5:3).

Peter continues with a general call for humility (5:6), based on humility under God. All are to submit to God and, as Micah 6:8 says, "to walk humbly with your God." But one who humbles himself will be raised up by God "in due time," which may mean at the last day. It all probably goes back to what Jesus said: "Whoever exalts himself will be humbled, and whoever humbles himself will be exalted" (Matt. 23:12). James wrote words almost identical to Peter's (James 4:10). The words of 5:7 are a precious assurance to people undergoing any kind of trial. Sometimes the only thing we can do is to rest in the Lord and wait patiently for Him. Peter is probably thinking of the words "Cast your cares on the Lord and he will sustain you; he will never let the righteous fall" (Ps. 55:22).

But the Christian life is not one only of passivity and quietism. There is a spiritual war to fight, and this is brought to view in 5:8, 9.

Once again, Peter sounds the bugle call for alertness and self-control that we heard in 1:13. The devil is at large and hungry. Peter's call to resist the devil is similar to that in James 4:7. Probably both Peter and James are drawing these ideas from Proverbs 3:34, interpreting "the proud" as, above all, the devil, as well as all who serve him. Christians can win in this battle because God is on their side, but they have to expect suffering and hardship. It is a worldwide war (5:9), so we need to fight bravely in our part of the battle line. (This verse shows that already the church had spread throughout the world known to the apostles. Compare Col. 1:6.)

Yes, God is fighting for us, and the battle will not be long (5:10). He who recruited us for His army is an invincible Leader. At this thought, Peter offers up another doxology (vs. 11) to the God of all grace, who gives grace to the humble.

■ Getting Into the Word

1 Peter 5:12-14

You need read this short postscript only once, but as you do so, try to visualize Peter and Silas as they close the letter. Then answer these questions:
1. What do the words of these concluding greetings tell us about Peter's purpose in writing the letter?
2. Silas was the Jewish name of Peter's literary assistant (vs. 12). His Greco-Roman name was Silvanus. There are many references to him in the book of Acts and Paul's letters. Find these references with the help of a concordance, and write a short biography of him.
3. Similarly, research and write a biography of Mark, who was also with Peter when he wrote (vs. 13).
4. It is generally agreed that the term *Babylon* in 5:13 refers not to literal Babylon but signifies Rome. Why does Peter refer to Rome in that way? Look up the places in the book of Revelation where *Babylon* is used symbolically. Refer to a concordance or the marginal notes in your Bible.

5. The "kiss of love" (vs. 14) is what Paul calls "a holy kiss." Find the five times that Paul refers to this custom. In what part of his letters do you find all the references? Where else in the New Testament do you find a kiss of greeting, and who gave it?

■ Exploring the Word

Goodbye

Peter refers to Silas (also called Silvanus) as his assistant in sending the letter (vs. 12). Literary assistants had a lot to do with putting an author's thoughts into good Greek, which included much more than fixing the spelling and grammar. Silas also might have been the one who was to deliver the letter, which may be the reason Peter made a point of recommending him as a "faithful brother." The addressees might never have seen Silas before, for Acts 16:6-8 tells us that when Paul and Silas had planned to go to Asia and Bithynia, the Spirit stopped them. Peter makes clear his reason for writing the letter (5:12), if it were not already obvious. He wanted to encourage them and keep them faithful.

"She who is in Babylon" (vs. 13) surely means their sister church in Rome. In Greek, the word for church (*ekklēsia*) is of the feminine grammatical gender. Even today we speak of "the sisterhood of churches," though the Christian community is called "the brotherhood" (2:17). In the opening greeting (1:1), Peter referred to his addressees as "God's elect" (or chosen). Here, he says that the Roman Christians are elect/chosen "together with you." This affirmation of solidarity was important, for the Roman Christians were facing the first official persecution, the fierce one instigated by Emperor Nero, and Peter suspected that something similar would soon befall the recipients of his letter.

Jewish writings were also using *Babylon* as a code word for Rome. This especially became the case after Rome destroyed Jerusalem in A.D. 70, the way Nebuchadnezzar of Babylon had done in 586 B.C. It is difficult to prove that this usage occurred before A.D. 70, but it is possible. Peter may very well have been the first to use this expression. In Rome, the emperor was trying to destroy the church, which is the temple of God (2:5), just as Nebuchadnezzar had destroyed the temple of Jerusalem.

Peter refers to Mark, who also sends greetings, as "my son." This does not mean, of course, that Peter was his literal father. It was a term of affection, just as Paul referred to Timothy as "my true son in the faith" (1 Tim. 1:2; compare 2 Tim. 1:2). The story of John Mark, cousin to Barnabas (Col. 4:10) is well known from the book of Acts and references to him in Paul's letters.

In Bible times, as in some cultures today, the kiss (5:14) was simply a form of friendly greeting, like our handshake. It could even be given insincerely, as when Judas kissed Jesus in greeting (Mark 14:44; Luke 22:47, 48). Perhaps with that possibility in mind, Peter specifically calls for a "kiss of love." The Greek word used here for love does not have a sexual connotation.

Finally, the letter closes with a peace greeting to match the one at the beginning of the letter (1:2; 5:14).

■ Applying the Word

1 Peter 4:12–5:14

1. Do the trials that I have suffered or am suffering make me a better person or a worse person? Do they lead me closer to God or away from Him? How can I relate to trials and difficulties in my life in a way that will result in the spiritual growth Peter outlines?

2. Do I have a firm commitment to the Lord and a confidence that in Him I will be victorious over trouble and evil? How can I be sure? What insight into self-examination does Peter's experience afford, as recorded in Mark 14:27-31? Why did Peter fail, and how did he recover? What does this teach me?

3. Have some of my troubles been such that I brought them on myself?

4. Have I ever been a busybody? Do I know someone who is? What can I do to warn that person against such a life? How can I balance refraining from meddling with showing genuine concern for people who need it?

5. Do I accept responsibility commensurate with my status and authority? Do I show humility and grace in filling the position I hold in the church?

6. Am I as willing to be a good follower as to be a good leader? How do I react when a church leader makes a mistake or a wrong decision? Why?

7. Have I really cast all my anxiety on the Lord, confident that He cares for me?

8. Am I standing firm in the faith, unflagging in my resistance to the works of the devil?

9. Do I serve the church faithfully, without undue concern for monetary pay?

■ Researching the Word

1. Using an exhaustive concordance, look up the word *glory*, and write a paragraph explaining what it is and who has it.

2. Make a search for the occurrences of the word *judgment*, and write a paragraph explaining its various meanings.

3. Research everything the Bible has to say about the devil/Satan.

4. In a good Bible dictionary or Bible encyclopedia, read the article on "Babylon."

■ Further Study of the Word

1. For a discussion of the typology involved in the judgment spoken of in 1 Peter 4:17, see G. Rice, *A Living Hope*, 114-117.

2. For helpful information on elders/bishops and other offices in the New Testament church, see the articles "Elders in the NT," "Presbyter," "Bishop," "Church Government," and

"Ministry" in G. W. Bromiley, ed., *The International Standard Bible Encyclopedia*. Also good are the articles "Elder" and "Bishop" in S. H. Horn, ed., *Seventh-day Adventist Bible Dictionary*, rev. ed.

3. For information about the Greek and Roman authors quoted in this and all preceding chapters, consult N. G. L. Hammond and H. H. Scullard, eds., *The Oxford Classical Dictionary*, 2nd ed.

PART TWO

2 Peter

Dangers
in the
Church

Introduction to
the Second Letter of Peter

As we move from 1 Peter to 2 Peter, the focus of concern for the church shifts from external menace to the internal dangers of loose living and false teaching. As you will soon see, that is not the only difference between Peter's two letters.

It would be ideal if you read through the twenty-five verses of Jude's short letter before reading 2 Peter, even though we are going to study Jude later. Then read the three chapters of 2 Peter, keeping in mind the don't-put-beans-up-your-nose principle of interpretation. As you read, keep in mind the following questions:

1. **How is 2 Peter different from 1 Peter?**
2. **How is 2 Peter related to Jude?**
3. **Why does 2 Peter say what it says? What are its main concerns? What and whom is it opposing? Why?**
4. **What are the main ideas of the letter?**
5. **What elements in 2 Peter especially speak to the needs of the church today and to your own spiritual condition? Write down in your notebook at least three such items.**

Now that you have read through Peter's second letter, seeking answers to some of the questions we have posed, you will doubtless have noticed that while much of it is similar to Jude, not much of 2 Peter is similar to 1 Peter. The differences of concern, of ideas, of style and vocabulary are even more pronounced in the original Greek. The terminology and way of expression in 2 Peter is, in fact, rather difficult and pretentious, with a definite tendency to use involved sentences and "fifty-cent words." Words such as *faith* are used with a different meaning than they carry in 1 Peter, and the use of Scripture is quite different. The author sometimes sounds like a second-generation Christian (3:2, 4) living at a time when the delay of Christ's second coming was beginning to be a problem for Christian faith.

Yet the letter clearly claims to be by Peter. Not only does the author identify himself as "Simon Peter" in the salutation (1:1), but he claims to be an eyewitness of Christ's transfiguration (vss. 16-18); he refers to Christ's prophecy that he would be martyred (vss. 13-15; compare John 21:19); he alludes to having sent a previous letter (3:1), probably 1 Peter; and, in general, he claims apostolic authority.

These two sets of facts have created a dilemma for Christian Bible students for almost as long as the history of the church. Perhaps no other book now in the New Testament encountered more hesitancy to accept it into the canon, though it was finally accepted. Doubts about its authenticity have persisted in modern times, with some scholars accusing the book of making an overdone effort to appear genuine (Sidebottom, 99) or calling its claim to be written by Peter "a transparent fiction," which people at the time it was written would not have misunderstood (Bauckham, 134, 158-160). After all, we know of several other apocryphal books that claimed to be written by Peter.

Though the arguments against Peter being the true author of this letter are often impressive, they are not compelling. The vast difference in literary style between 1 Peter and 2 Peter is not surprising when we understand the role and function of literary assistants. Clearly, someone other than Silas worked with Peter on his second letter. The difference in tone and ideas is understandable in the light of the difference of purpose and concern. Besides, not all of the concerns are so different. In the second letter, one of Peter's main concerns is about a libertine theology based partly on a misunderstanding of Paul's message of Christian liberty, a concern anticipated in 1 Peter 2:15, 16, though from a slightly different perspective. We therefore take the position that the authority of the apostle Peter stands behind this letter in such a way that it was not wrong for it to present itself as his letter.

Peter must have sent this letter out some time after his first letter (3:1) and very close to the time of his execution in Rome (1:14). It was not only Peter's last letter but his last testament, in the same way that 2 Timothy was Paul's last testament (compare 2 Tim. 4:6-8).

Purpose of 2 Peter

Among the people to whom Peter sent this letter, the fervent expectation of Christ's imminent second advent was in danger of fading. Besides, most of them had come out of a pagan cultural background—suggested by Peter's speaking of their escaping from the corruption in the world (1:4)—and some of them may have been embarrassed by Christian peculiarities that kept them from participating in many of the activities of their former friends and associates (as we saw in 1 Peter). The primitive apostolic message of repentance and godly living in preparation for the Parousia may have begun to sound untenably out of date—unsophisticated and legalistic. Apparently a significant group felt that Paul's message set them free from keeping the law (3:14-18). The behavioral rules of the church, and even of society, they thought, concerned merely "externals" and could be disregarded by intelligent Christians (2:2). The important thing about religion was theologizing, what you know, not how you live—creed, not deed. These ideas were promoted by people whom Peter calls "false teachers" (2:1).

Who were these teachers whom Peter opposed so vehemently? They may have simply been young "liberals," rebelling against the authority of their elders. They may have been former pagans who had been immersed in some of the popular philosophies of the time, particularly Epicureanism (compare Acts 17:18). The Epicureans were generally thought to be rather skeptical and hedonistic. They did not believe that the gods interfered in human affairs, and they taught that the great objective of life was to seek pleasure and avoid pain. They even came to overlook the fact that their founder, Epicurus, had warned against indulgent excess and sensuous living, because sooner or later, the result is misery, and that he advocated the quiet life of the mind as producing the most lasting pleasure. To the Epicureans, the ideas of God coming to earth and of a final judgment did not make sense.

But the false teachers whom Peter describes seem to go beyond such a muddled mixing of Epicurean philosophy with Christian belief, though that may have been the background of many who responded to their ideas. The fact that Peter calls them teachers implies that they were propagating a definite doctrine or ideology. That is why many Bible students have supposed that Peter's opponents were spreading an early form of Gnosticism.

Gnosticism comes from the Greek word *gnosis*, which means "knowledge." That is what Gnostics thought they had. What kind of knowledge? Above all, knowledge of themselves—where they came from, why they were here, and where they were going—divine secrets they claimed had been revealed to them. Paul referred to the Gnostics when he said: "Turn away from godless chatter and the opposing ideas of what is falsely called knowledge [*gnosis*], which some have professed and in so doing have wandered from the faith" (1 Tim. 6:20, 21). Gnosticism is not just an ancient heresy but a state of mind that emerges again and again. Perhaps the latest manifestation of it in our culture is the New Age movement.

No one now knows just how Gnosticism began in New Testament times, though the ancient church fathers said it was begun by Simon the Magician, of whom we read in Acts 8:9-24. Others spoke of Nicolaus or Nicolas (see Acts 6:5), founder of the Nicolaitans (Rev. 2:6). We know much more about how Gnosticism developed in the second century, but we can assume that many of its features were already beginning to develop in the time of the apostles. Paul (Acts 20:29, 30) as well as Peter warned against Gnostic gurus who would arise within the church.

Gnosticism, like Christianity, was a countercultural way of thinking. Both would attract disillusioned people who would be inclined to think the two were compatible. Like the "hippies" of the 1960s, their cry could have been: "Stop the world! I want to get off!" They also wanted to intellectualize Christianity by infusing it with the ideas of Plato, so pervasive in the ancient world. They wanted to correct the "Jewish" aspect of Christianity by interpreting it in the light of the received philosophies of the day. In this they thought they had the support of Paul's theology, for they took some of their inspiration from the way they understood a few of his more unguarded statements in Galatians, Romans, and perhaps Colossians (in spite of the fact that the latter epistle was likely directed against an early form of Gnosticism).

The Gnostics broke up into many groups, each following its own teacher; and each teacher had his own system of theology. But certain elements were common to most of them, and it will be helpful to examine what these were.

Their theology was one of radical dualism. They made an absolute separation between spirit and matter, corresponding to light and darkness. They believed that everything spiritual is good, and everything physical is evil, including the material world and our bodies. This world is the realm of darkness, an evil mess. Whoever created it was a bungler. There is a High God, ruler of the realm of light beyond the material universe, who had nothing to do with creating this mess. The creator of the world was an inferior or fallen god who botched things terribly. (The Gnostics interpreted Genesis 1 to 3 in the light of the other creation story current at the time, the one in Plato's *Timaeus*, according to which the material world was made by an intermediate deity called the demiurge.) The Highest God is hidden from us, and we can know Him only through revelation.

This world is ruled by "principalities and powers," strange supernatural beings who rule by fate, which enslaves people by natural law and the Mosaic law. The material universe is a vast prison, and its innermost dungeon is the earth.

Humankind has a twofold origin. Our body and soul (the appetites, emotions, and passions) were created either by the principalities and powers or by the inferior creator god. But the human spirit is a spark or portion of the Divine, which somehow got broken off and fell into the world and is imprisoned in the body. "Who cast me into this stinking body?" cried the Gnostics. The spirit is enclosed by the body and soul as by a straightjacket, asleep, intoxicated, ignorant. Awakening and liberation come by knowledge (*gnosis*).

Humans' spiritual self is foreign to this world, and we must strive to achieve release and liberation. Then the spirit will return to the realm of light. Equipped with *gnosis*, the spirit after death soars upward, shedding its soulish "vestments," and finally purified, it is reunited with the divine substance that God is: the rays of light return to the Divine from which they were once separated. Then the Deity becomes whole again, for the missing pieces of light and spirit are returned, and God becomes All in All.

The revelation of this saving knowledge, said the Gnostics, was brought by a divine Messenger, who was sent to retrieve the detached portions of the Light. That, said most Gnostics, is who Jesus was. He did not come to die, but to enlighten. Because the physical body is evil, He could not possibly have been literally incarnated. He only seemed to have a body, and He only seemed to be crucified. It was all just a trick played on the stupid creator god. When the material universe is deprived of all the pieces of light that have been imprisoned in it, then it will come to an end (so taught some of the Gnostic gurus).

"Spiritual things are spiritually discerned," quoted the Gnostics, who believed that only they were spiritual. One school of Gnostic thought taught that humankind is divided into three classes: material people (non-Christians), soulish people (ordinary Christians), and spiritual people (Gnostic Christians). If people did not understand or accept the Gnostic teaching, the reason was that they were not spiritual. A Gnostic is like an eagle who is hatched from his egg in a brood of chickens and does not know that he is an eagle. The Gnostic teachers saw it as their task to awaken and enlighten the slumbering spirits and to make them aware that they were eagles. (The New Testament teaches that no one is born an eagle, except Jesus. We are all by nature chickens!)

They believed that Gnostics, the spiritual people, are set apart from the great mass of humankind. They had contempt for all earthly ties and also for the body. Morally, this theology led to two opposite extremes. The majority of Gnostics were ascetic. They showed their contempt for physical existence by extreme abstinence (see Col. 2:21;

1 Tim. 4:3). But their ideas could work the other way; some thought they could deliberately abuse their bodies by licentious indulgence! If the body is evil or unimportant, what does it matter what we do with it? Simon the Magician is reported to have promoted sexual promiscuity as a duty among his followers. In the early second century, an example of this tendency was the Gnostic teacher Carpocrates. He taught his followers that they must experience everything, even wicked things, in order to be saved from reincarnation into another body after death.

Then there was the early Gnostic group called the Ophites or Naasenes (from the Greek word for *serpent*, *ophis*, or the Hebrew word for *serpent*, *nahash*), who revered the serpent as the bringer of enlightenment. They were against the Old Testament and the God of the Old Testament, whom they saw as the stupid creator god. When the serpent in Eden told Eve, "God knows that when you eat of it your eyes will be opened, and you will be like God, knowing good and evil" (Gen. 3:5), he was right; the Creator wanted to keep humans' spirit in ignorance! The Ophites regarded all the villains of the Old Testament (the serpent, Cain, Korah, Dathan, Abiram, etc.) as heroes. They went deliberately opposite to everything in the Jewish Scriptures.

If you have found all this shocking, and yet fascinating or even attractive, then you can begin to understand why Peter sent his second letter, and perhaps even why he had it written in the style in which we find it. The Gnostic teachers were fond of using impressive-sounding theological language and of talking about things like knowledge and escape from the corruption of the world. You can also understand why the early church considered Gnostic thinking to be its most dangerous internal threat. Had it not been for the Gnostics, the very concepts of orthodoxy and heresy might never have developed, for the early church was remarkably diverse. But Gnosticism was just too much to take, especially because Gnostic behavior gave Christianity a bad name.

Peter's purpose was to oppose these pseudointellectuals, whether they were early Gnostics (as seems probable to me) or simply young rebels who naively thought that they were sophisticated and advocated a Christianity more in tune with fashionable philosophical trends. He sought to oppose them by trying to express himself on their wavelength, writing in their idiom. Using the Hellenistic mode of thought and expression (Hellenism, the imitation of Greek customs and ways of thinking, was the modernity of that time), Peter set forth the case for the apostolic teaching about morality and eschatology.

His opponents were antinomians, ridiculing the law of God, and they were trying to justify their libertinism by appealing to the name of Paul. They cast doubt on the doctrine of the second coming of Christ, the last judgment, and the end of the world by fire. If salvation comes by knowledge and the enlightened spirit returns from the world and body to God (of which it is a portion) at death, then who needs God to return to the world? And if there is no judgment (to paraphrase Dostoevski), then all things are permitted.

Peter meets such arguments head on. His purpose is to oppose the (possibly) Gnostic error and defend the biblical and apostolic truth (3:2). He presents the *real* knowledge and the *right* way to escape the corruption in the world.

The Structure of 2 Peter

Before we can discover the structure of 2 Peter, we must establish its relation to Jude. That is why I asked you to read Jude first. If you compared the two letters carefully, you noticed that the middle part of 2 Peter (2:1–3:3) corresponds very closely to Jude. We can set it out in this table:

	2 Peter	Jude
False teachers denying the Lord	2:1-3	4
Fallen angels cast into darkness	2:4	6
Sodom and Gomorrah	2:6	7
Lusting, rejecting authority	2:10	8
Slandering heavenly beings	2:10, 11	8
Angel not reviling back	2:11	9
Like irrational animals	2:12	10

Blemishes, carousing	2:13	12
Balaam's way	2:15	11
Storm clouds, darkness	2:17	12, 13
Boasts, lust	2:18	16
Apostolic predictions	3:2	17
Scoffers in the last days	3:3	18

You can clearly see that not only the ideas but the sequence of ideas is the same. Such a close correspondence cannot possibly be a coincidence, so some kind of literary dependence is certain.

There are three possibilities: (1) Peter used Jude; (2) Jude used Peter; or (3) Peter and Jude both used some common source. For persuasive reasons, we can eliminate the second possibility. The third option is a real possibility, but an unnecessary solution. I believe that the best explanation is that 2 Peter 2:1 to 3:3 is a paraphrase of Jude, adapting Jude's points to the situation Peter was addressing. Peter, or Peter's literary assistant, has skillfully worked this paraphrase into the letter, leading up to it with a section stressing the importance of godly living and the trustworthiness of the apostolic and prophetic witnesses. The paraphrase is followed by another section defending the apostolic teaching about eschatology and giving some concluding warnings. The whole is framed by similar blessings in 1:2 and 3:18, wishing upon the readers grace and the knowledge of God and Jesus Christ.

This gives us our outline, which can correspond with the three chapters into which our Bibles divide the letter. While it is true that 3:1-3 is still part of the paraphrase taken from Jude, it serves as the lead-in to the last section, so we are justified in making it part of that. We suggest the following outline of 2 Peter:

   I. Starting With the Positive (1:1-21)
      A. Greetings to Fellow Believers (1:1, 2)
      B. Making Certain of Salvation (1:3-11)
      C. Making Certain of the Message (1:12-21)
  II. Warning Against False Teachers (2:1-22)
      A. The Certainty of Judgment Upon Evildoers (2:1-10a)
      B. The Character and Destiny of the False Teachers (2:10b-22)

III. What to Do While the Lord Delays His Coming (3:1-18)
   A. Warning Against Scoffers (3:1-7)
   B. How to Prepare for the Day of the Lord (3:8-16)
   C. Summing Up and Praising (3:17, 18)

Major Themes in 2 Peter

Many of the things Peter says, and the way he says them, would be especially appropriate in dealing with people who were tempted by Gnostic teachings.

1. Peter speaks often of *knowledge*. But to Peter, saving knowledge is not knowledge of the Gnostic myth about one's self; rather, saving knowledge is the knowledge of God and of Jesus Christ. Peter uses the word *gnosis* in 1:5, 6, and 3:18. In 1:2, 3, 8, and 2:20 he uses the word *epignosis*, which means the same thing.

2. In contrast with the Gnostic notion of spirituality by the supposed discovery of what you really are, Peter has much to say about *true spirituality*. The real way to participate in the divine nature and to escape the corruption of the world is not through contempt for all earthly ties but by cultivating legitimate relationships and developing character and morality (1:3-11). Peter gives no indication that by our origin we have a spark of divinity within us. Participation in the Deity is not something discovered, but something acquired.

3. Accordingly, there is an important emphasis on *moral living* (1:5-8; 3:11, 14). One of the most distressing things about the false teachers was that their way of life brought Christianity into disrepute (2:2).

4. Peter promotes *confidence* in the teaching of the apostles and prophets (1:16-21; 3:1, 2, 15), which had been discredited by the false teachers.

5. The other side of the coin is the central theme of the letter: opposition to *false teaching* (2:1-3, 10-21) and to *skepticism* (3:3, 4) and *apostasy* (2:20-22; 3:16, 17).

6. Because the apostolic *eschatology* was under attack, Peter stresses the certainty of the Day of the Lord (3:8-10), the final judgment (2:3b-10a, 13a; 3:6-11), and the new earth (3:13).

7. Along with all this, Peter reminds his readers of *God's patience* (3:9, 15).

8. At the same time, Peter calls for *heedfulness* on the part of believers so as not to fall (1:10; 2:20; 3:17). Peter wants to discourage a false sense of security such as might grow out of the Gnostic teaching that spiritual people are such by origin, regardless of what they do, and need only to discover their true natures. He also gives no comfort to those who hold to the idea that once we are saved, we shall be always saved.

For Further Reading

1. You may want to pursue further the question of the authenticity of 2 Peter—whether Peter in some sense is the true author or whether the letter is pseudepigraphical. Arguments for its pseudonymity are advanced by R. J. Bauckham (an evangelical believer), *Jude, 2 Peter*, 131-163; J. H. Elliott in D. N. Freedman, ed., *The Anchor Bible Dictionary*, 5:283; and by E. M. Sidebottom, *James, Jude, 2 Peter*, 99, 100. Petrine authorship is supported by E. M. B. Green, *2 Peter Reconsidered*; N. Hillyer, *1 and 2 Peter, Jude*, 9-11; and S. J. Kistemaker, *Exposition of the Epistles of Peter and of the Epistle of Jude*, 213-219.

2. The relation of 2 Peter to Jude is dealt with in nearly all the good commentaries, most of which support the position that Peter paraphrased Jude. On that side, Sidebottom, Bauckham, and (apparently) Kistemaker give good discussions. Hillyer goes for the position that both Peter and Jude used a common written source.

3. There is a vast literature about Gnosticism. See the article and bibliography by K. Rudolph in D. N. Freedman, ed., *The Anchor Bible Dictionary*, 2:1033-140, and the one by A. M. Renwick in G. W. Bromiley, ed., *The International Standard Bible Encyclopedia*, 2:484-490. A good collection of Gnostic writings is found in B. Layton, *The Gnostic Scriptures*.

4. Bauckham, 154-157, thinks that the opponents against whom Peter argues were young liberal rebels; and Elliott, 5:285, argues that they were former Epicureans.

CHAPTER FIVE

Starting With the Positive

2 Peter 1:1-21

Peter begins this letter with the usual greeting (1:1, 2), a greeting with some special details that distinguish it from the greeting in chapter 1 of First Peter. Like that greeting, it anticipates some themes he will develop.

The ideas that Peter develops first in this section are positive and encouraging ones. Jude, whose letter I believe Peter used, said that he had wanted to write about "the salvation we share" (Jude 3) but instead, he immediately launched into a polemic against the false teachers. Peter avoids repeating Jude's omission by reserving his polemic against the false teachers until after he has expounded upon salvation in 1:3-11. It is refreshing that Peter wants to present truth before denouncing error.

In 1:12-15 Peter introduces his last testament, which conforms to the pattern of other religious testaments of the time (see Bauckham, 131-135, 194). He says that he expects to die soon and that he wants his teaching to be remembered. He then defends the trustworthiness of that teaching, appealing to his experience as an eyewitness of the Lord's glory (1:16-18) and insisting on the truth of Bible prophecy (1:19-21).

■ Getting Into the Word

2 Peter 1

Read the first two verses thoughtfully, comparing them to the first two verses of 1 Peter, chapter 1. Notice especially what is added to the greeting in 2 Peter. Review what chapter 1 of

this book said about the greetings in 1 Peter. Then read the rest of 2 Peter, chapter 1, always asking the question, Why did Peter say this?

Finally, answer the following questions, referring to a concordance or other helps when appropriate. Write your answers in a notebook you keep for 2 Peter.

1. The author gives his name more fully in 2 Peter than in 1 Peter. Where else in the New Testament do you find him called Simon? Where else do you find the combination Simon Peter? What pattern, if any, do you find in the usage?

2. Similarly, the author of 2 Peter uses a longer title for himself, not simply "an apostle" but "a servant and apostle." In what other New Testament epistles do the authors identify themselves as "a servant of Jesus Christ"?

3. Peter makes a theological statement about the addressees in verse 1. What is the meaning of that statement? What are its implications?

4. To the usual mention of "grace and peace" in the greeting, Peter adds "knowledge" (1:2). Why do you think he does this? Where else in the New Testament do you find mention of knowledge as a saving virtue? What does the rest of chapter 1 imply about knowledge? List and explain your findings.

5. What do you think 1:4 means by its reference to participating in the divine nature? Are there any similar statements elsewhere in the Bible? In what sense does this phrase mean that human beings can become like God? What does the immediate context imply as to how we can participate in the divine nature?

6. What reasons can you detect for the sequence of virtues listed in 1:5-7?

7. What do you think Peter means by "calling" (1:3, 10)? What does he mean by "falling" (1:10, 3:17; compare 2:20)?

8. What verse(s) in this chapter indicate the reasons prompting Peter to send this letter? Summarize those reasons in your notebook.

9. Why do you think Peter makes the point he does in 1:16?

Read the descriptions of Christ's transfiguration in Matthew, Mark, and Luke. What does the immediate context of the transfiguration account in each Gospel tell us about its significance? Compare your findings with 2 Peter 1:16-18. What is Peter's point here?

10. **Discuss the implications of 1:19, 20 for an understanding of inspiration.**

■ Exploring the Word

The Address on the Envelope

As you saw in the case of 1 Peter, this letter identifies the sender as well as the addressees at the very beginning of the letter (1:1), as was the custom in ancient times. We need not repeat here the information found in chapter 1 of this book; what draws our attention here are the differences from Peter's earlier letter.

The author identifies himself not just as Peter, but as Simon Peter. Actually, the NIV obscures the fact that Peter uses a special spelling of the name Simon—Symeon—which reflects the Hebrew pronunciation. That special spelling for Peter's name is found only here and in Acts 15:14. Just as there was a regular Greek form (Simon) and a Hebrew form (Symeon) of his real name, similarly there were Greek (*Petros*) and Hebrew-Aramaic (*Kepha*) forms of the nickname Jesus gave him. The curious thing here is that he mixes the Hebrew given name with the Greek nickname, and he does it in a letter sent to churches that were mainly Gentile. I think this usage is a nice touch supporting authentic Petrine authorship. If another author had wanted to imitate 1 Peter deliberately, he likely would have copied the name used there. But by using a Palestinian name, Peter subtly reminds his readers that his experience goes back to the beginnings of the church.

This letter shows a fondness for using two words instead of one. We see that again in the author's title: "a servant and apostle of Jesus Christ"—1 Peter only has "an apostle of Jesus Christ." The word used here for servant (*doulos*), of course, means "slave." Jude had titled himself "a servant of Jesus Christ" (Jude 1), and Peter could have picked it up from there. James used only the title "servant" (James 1:1), and Paul also sometimes used it alone (Phil. 1:1) or connected with God (Titus 1:1). In the Old Testament, *servant* in relation to a deity meant a worshiper (i.e., servant of Baal, servant of the Lord). In the New Testament, it meant that and more. A servant of Jesus Christ regards Him as Lord and does His bidding.

Peter does not identify the addressees as specifically here as he does in his first letter. From 3:1 we might infer that they were the same people who received the first letter. Here, he rather identifies them as "those who through the righteousness of our God and Savior Jesus Christ have received a faith as precious as ours" (1:1b). The word that the NIV translates "as precious as" could also be rendered "of equal privilege" or "of equal standing."

At first blush, this seems an odd thing to say. Is not all faith equal? And whose faith is he talking about when he says "ours"? He is probably talking about the faith of the apostles, who had been personally associated with Jesus. Peter is saying to these Gentile second-generation believers that their faith is just as good as that of those who had seen the Lord on earth. We remember what Jesus said to Thomas: "Because you have seen me, you have believed; blessed are those who have not seen and yet have believed" (John 20:29). Notice, also, that those to whom Peter is writing "received" their faith "through the righteousness of our God." No one and no generation can boast of achieving something they have received as a gift, by the grace of God. The "righteousness of our God" here means His fairness and impartiality. When it comes to saving faith, Christ's disciples and apostles had no advantage over any later generation. (However, 1 Peter 1:10, 11 suggests that earlier generations in Old Testament times in a sense were less privileged, though not less capable of being saved.) Because all believers have an equal faith, they share a common salvation (compare Jude 3).

Faith in this verse means something like what it means in Jude, and that is different from what it means in 1:5. Here, faith apparently means the object or content of what we believe, rather than the act of believing itself. It is *what* we believe, as when we speak of "the Christian faith."

We must not pass too quickly over the phrase "our God and Savior Jesus Christ" in the first verse. The Greek structure strongly suggests that God and Jesus are the same, that Jesus is here called God. (The same is true in Titus 2:13; compare 1 John 5:20.) In the next verse, that identity is not so clear, and it is possible to make a distinction there.

Perhaps the most striking difference between Peter's greeting in his second letter and that in his first is the addition of "through the knowledge of God and of Jesus Christ our Lord" (1:2). As we have already noted, *knowledge* is a very important word in 2 Peter. In the NIV *knowledge* or *knowing* appears seven times, while *faith* is used only twice.

There are two reasons for that, based on Peter's strategy. First, Peter wants to preempt the favorite word of the false teachers. He wants to nail down the fact that the knowledge that saves is not the Gnostic myth about who we are, but the knowledge of who Jesus is. Second, when false teaching is the issue, knowledge takes priority over faith, because the problem is not unbelief but gullibility. The issue is not *whether* you believe, but *what* you believe! In our emphasis upon saving faith, we must not forget that we also need saving knowledge, the kind of knowledge Jesus spoke of when He said, "Now this is eternal life: that they may know you, the only true God, and Jesus Christ, whom you have sent" (John 17:3). The kind of knowledge spoken of here is not theoretical knowledge, though that has its place, but personal acquaintance.

Making Certain of Salvation

Peter has now finished the formalities, but they were more than formalities, because they introduced the subject he now turns to. He has spoken of knowledge and of God and Jesus our Lord. That knowledge is Peter's message, and he is now going to explain it in 1:3-11. His presentation has three parts. First, he tells what God has done for us (vss. 3, 4). Second, he tells what we should do for God (vss. 5-9). Third, he tells about the reward of faithfulness at the end (vss. 10, 11).

It is not clear whether "his divine power" (vs. 3) refers to God's power or to Christ's (though it would hardly have been necessary to mention that God's power is divine), and perhaps that is just as well. God's power comes to us through Christ, and Christ's power is God's power. The important thing is that His power "has given us everything we need for life and godliness." Here is another case in which Peter uses two words to express one thought (a literary device called *hendiadys*, from a Greek word meaning literally "one thing through two"). *Life and godliness* simply means "godly life." Godliness, or piety, is mentioned four times in 2 Peter (1:3, 6, 7; 3:11). It is also an important word in the letters Paul sent to Timothy and Titus. It means "the respect for God's will and the moral way of life which are inseparable from the proper religious attitude to God" (Bauckham, 178).

That which activates this abundant gift of "everything we need" for godliness is our knowledge of Christ, who called us (1:3). Peter is going to have some important things to say about this calling later on. The palpable response to the call was conversion manifested in baptism. The call came to us through Christ's "own glory and goodness," another hendiadys of Peter's. The word translated "goodness" when ascribed to a hero or a god really meant "wonder-working effectiveness." Ascribed to a human being, it meant "excellence."

Along with the call, He "has given us his very great and precious promises" (1:4), which could also mean that He has given what was promised. These could be Old Testament promises or promises Jesus gave while He was on earth. The exact time when these promises were given is not as important as their practical realization "so that through them you may participate in the divine nature and escape the corruption in the world caused by evil desires." Again Peter preempts an expression of the false teachers and refills it with true meaning. Greek philosophy taught that human beings have a spiritual part that is akin to the immortal gods, totally separate from their material, bodily part. Picking up on that, the Gnostic teachers said that the spirits of some people are pieces of the divine that got broken off somehow and will eventually return. So Gnostic believers, they said, are partakers of the divine nature by their very origin. At death they will leave this corrupt world and their stinking bodies, in which they have been imprisoned.

Seizing upon the very expressions the false teachers were bandying about, Peter refills them with correct meaning and uses them as a vehicle for inspired truth. But in what sense can human beings participate in the divine nature? This expression is found nowhere else in the New Testament, although some references approach it (Rom. 8:15-18; 1 John 3:1, 2), and Peter himself had said earlier that we will "share in the glory to be revealed" (1 Pet. 5:1). Systematic theologians make a useful distinction between the communicable attributes of God and His incommunicable attributes. The "incommunicable attributes" are those that created beings can never share, such as self-existence, omnipotence, omniscience, and omnipresence. The communicable attributes are those that He imparts to those who are willing, such as goodness, love, mercy, and long-suffering—in other words, His moral attributes. It is clear from 1:5-7 that the moral attributes of God are, in fact, what Peter has in mind when he speaks of sharing the divine nature. That is quite a different idea from what the Gnostic teachers were saying. They were teaching that people need only discover the divine nature that is already theirs by their origin. Peter says that the moral nature is a gift from God that must be developed. Furthermore, the "corruption in the world" is not caused by materiality, as the Gnostics taught, but by evil desires (vs. 4). We escape it not by abusing the body, but by rightly using it.

In 1:5-9, Peter spells out the moral development he is referring to, making use of two literary features current at that time. One feature is the virtue list, which is the opposite of a vice list such as we saw in 1 Peter 2:1 (see chapter 2). Such lists were common in the moral literature of Peter's day. They were used not only in Jewish and Christian teaching but also by pagan moralists, especially Stoic philosophers. In the New Testament, we find such lists in 2 Corinthians 6:6-7a; Galatians 5:22, 23; Ephesians 4:2, 3, 32; 5:1, 2, 9; Philippians 4:8; Colossians 3:12; 1 Timothy 3:2-4, 8-12; 4:12; 6:11, 18; 2 Timothy 2:22-25; 3:10; Titus 1:8; 2:2-10; Hebrews 7:26; 1 Peter 3:8; and here in 2 Peter 1:5-7.

The other literary feature that Peter uses is called *sorites* (from the Greek word *soros*, "heap"). The dictionary defines it thus: "An argument consisting of propositions so arranged that the predicate of any one forms the subject of the next and the conclusion unites the subject of the first proposition with the predicate of the last" (*Merriam Webster's Collegiate Dictionary*, 1122). What we find in 2 Peter conforms at least to the first part of the definition. It is like a chain of links. There is something somewhat like it in Romans 5:3-5.

"Make every effort to add," says Peter (1:5). The idea that human effort is involved in salvation is difficult for some Christians, who feel that it runs counter to Paul's gospel of salvation by grace alone through faith. The relation of works to faith has been a perennial point of debate. There is an inescapable paradox here, that while the Christian life is one of restfulness, it is also a battle and a march. "Make every effort to enter through the narrow door," said Jesus (Luke 13:24).

The fact is that Peter traces everything back to divine power (1:3), which agrees fully with what Paul said: "Continue to work out your salvation with fear and trembling, for it is God who works in you to will and to act according to his good purpose" (Phil. 2:12, 13). We are simply dealing with the necessary response to God's grace, which is to cooperate with it. We are to be colaborers with God. When we come to God, we sing, "Just as I am, without one plea, but that Thy blood was shed for me." But after that we sing, "I would be, dear Saviour, wholly Thine." A spiritually alive person grows in character, because he wants to please his Lord and represent Him aright.

A citizen of France is French even if he does not act French, but if he does not so act, he denies his citizenship. He may be guilty of treason, in a way that a German would not be, if he did not act French. A disobedient child remains his parent's child, but his behavior will have consequences. Peter's concept is that a Christian can forsake his Christianity (2:20) and thus demonstrate that his connection with God's grace and power is severed. Such a person has given up his calling and has "fallen" (compare 1:10; 3:17).

Peter's list of eight virtues begins with faith (1:5), for that is the beginning of all Christian life, the first rung of the ladder. It is the initial response to the gospel.

To faith we must add "goodness," as the NIV weakly translates it. This is the same word we saw in 1:3, but here it means moral excellence in general.

The third virtue to add is knowledge (*gnosis*), but not the kind the Gnostics babbled about. It means the knowledge of God in Jesus Christ and of the things of God, including wisdom and understanding. Christianity is not—or should not be—anti-intellectual. Jesus told us to love the Lord our God with all our mind (Matt. 22:37).

The fourth virtue is self-control. Pagan philosophers also preached self-discipline and temperance, but they did not have a clue about how to achieve it. Christians know that the only way to self-control is God-control.

Fifth is perseverance (the word could also be translated steadfastness or endurance). This was a virtue much needed in the face of persecution, trial, and temptation. James regarded it as a cardinal virtue (James 1:2, 3), and Peter in his earlier letter considered the endurance of unjust punishment part of a Christian's calling (1 Pet. 2:20, 21).

The sixth step adds godliness, already referred to in 1:3. One definition is "putting loyalty to God above all else" (Hillyer, 166).

Seventh is brotherly kindness (*philadelphia*). Peter had included this among the virtues in 1 Peter 3:8. Paul had also stressed its importance (Rom. 12:10; 1 Thess. 4:9; Heb. 13:1). It simply means the special affection we should have for fellow believers.

The eighth and crowning virtue is love (*agapē*). For Paul also, it was the greatest virtue (1 Cor. 13:13); in fact, he considered it the fulfillment of the law (Rom. 13:10). Jesus defined perfection in terms of this virtue, loving even our enemies spontaneously, continuously, and unconditionally just as God does (Matt. 5:43-48). When you develop this virtue, therefore, you really do "participate in the divine nature" (1:4).

We cannot say of these virtues that either you have them or you don't. It is possible to have them in varying degrees, and the great enterprise of character building involves having them in "increasing measure" (1:8). We must keep on developing them in order not to be "ineffective and unproductive"—the Greek literally means "workless and fruitless." The New Testament has much to say about bearing fruit (Mark 4:20; John 15:5-8; Gal. 5:22-26). The first business of Christians is not to *do* but to *be*. Those who *are* abiding in Christ will produce. There must be life before there can be action. But there is no such thing as having these virtues without their being shown in good works. Paul said, "The only thing that counts is faith expressing itself through love" (Gal. 5:6).

Verse 9 shows clearly that Peter is addressing baptized Christians. A Christian who is not developing Christian character is "nearsighted and blind" (another hendiadys, and a rather awkward one—how can one be nearsighted and blind at the same time?), of course meaning spiritually blind. Furthermore, he "has forgotten that he has been cleansed from his past sins" by conversion and baptism. In 2:20 Peter will say that a person in such a condition is even worse off than if he or she had never been cleansed in the first place! It is important to remember the covenant we made when we were baptized (compare Rom. 6:1-14). It is also important to remember that it is not enough to avoid sin; we must also embrace virtue. One cannot be done without the other.

That is a Christian's "calling and election" (another hendiadys!), and "if you do these things, you will never fall" (1:10). The clear implication is that falling is a possibility. There are those who claim that once a person is saved, he will always be saved (the doctrine of "the perseverance of the saints"), but that doctrine finds scant support here, and even less later in the letter (2:20; 3:17). Advocates of the doctrine may argue that if someone falls, it shows that he never really was saved in the first place. But the bottom line is the same: "Make your calling and election sure" (1:10).

The final result of faithfulness will be "a rich welcome into the eternal kingdom of our Lord and Savior Jesus Christ" (vs. 11). That is the eschatological part of Peter's message. The kingdom of God and of His Christ is the most central of all New Testament doctrines. It is different from the Gnostic idea of reabsorption into the All. Peter may very well be remembering Jesus' words in the parable of the sheep and the goats (Matt. 25:31-46). At the judgment the King will say to those who have practiced the benevolent virtues: "Come, you who are blessed by my Father; take your inheritance, the kingdom prepared for you since the creation of the world" (Matt. 25:34). What a welcome!

Making Certain of the Message

Peter now tells us his reason for sending this letter. It is his last testament. He expects to die soon (1:14), and he wants to make sure that the people remember the true teaching given by him and the other apostles. In harmony with the conventions of other such testaments, both in and out of the Bible, he will also be making predictions and warning of dangers. Paul did these same things in 2 Timothy.

Peter begins this section tactfully by saying that his readers already know these things and "are firmly established in the truth" (1:12). But he is not so confident in their doctrinal firmness that he refrains from reminding them! Indeed, in the Christian walk, it is often the case that we need to be reminded of what we already know. Peter then talks of his impending death in terms of putting off the "tent of this body" (vs. 13). We should not make too much of this metaphor, though it is somewhat reminiscent of the literal meaning of John 1:14, "The Word became flesh and *tented* among us." A tent is a temporary dwelling, a fitting picture of the briefness of this life.

Peter alludes to the fact that his death had been announced to him by "our Lord Jesus Christ" (1:14), perhaps referring to the incident recorded in John 21:18, 19. The word he uses for *departure* in verse 15 is *exodus*. The only other place in the New Testament where this word is used for death is Luke 9:31, in the description of Christ's transfiguration, which ties this paragraph to the next one (vss. 16-18). (It was first used in this sense in the apocryphal book, The Wisdom of Solomon.)

Peter promises to make use of whatever time he has left "to see that after my departure you will always be able to remember these things" (vs. 15). He may not be referring only to this letter but also to the Gospel of Mark. According to early Christian tradition, Mark composed his Gospel by writing the things he heard from Peter.

At this point, Peter begins to defend his testimony and that of the other apostles. "We did not follow cleverly invented stories" (vs. 16), he declares. The NIV word *stories* translates the Greek word *mythoi,* "myths." In ancient times this word had both a positive and a negative connotation, like our word *fable*. Positively, it could mean a story about the gods that should not be taken literally but that contained a religious or philosophical truth. Such was the claim for Plato's creation story in the *Timaeus*. The Gnostics invented myths of this sort to explain their doctrine. These were complicated philosophical tales attempting to explain the mystery of how the dark material world came out of the divine realm of light, how evil came from pure Good (see Layton, 12-18), how spirits fell into bodies. The myth was in the form of a story, but it made no pretense of being literal history. In fact, the Gnostics had no interest at all in history.

In ancient times the word *myth* also could have a negative connotation, just as it usually has today, meaning an untrue fiction. Peter is obviously using the word in a negative sense in 1:16, but what exactly is his point? He may be shrewdly making two points at the same time. On the one hand, he is saying that the apostolic message is not a fiction but is true history. It may well be that some of Peter's opponents were charging that the whole story about Jesus was made up. On the other hand, Peter may be jabbing a needle into the Gnostic myth that the false teachers were propagating and that stood in contrast to the sober account the apostles professed to give.

Peter is particularly concerned to defend the doctrines of the second coming and the judgment. In 1:16-18 he is clearly describing his experience as an eyewitness of Christ's transfiguration (Matt. 17:1-8; Mark 9:1-8; Luke 9:28-36). He understood this as a foretaste and assurance of the second coming of Christ in glory. The transfiguration was proof that the apostles were not lying "when we told you about the power and coming of our Lord Jesus Christ" (vs. 16).

They were "eyewitnesses of his majesty" (vs. 16). That was a major function of the apostles, to stand as eyewitnesses. When they chose a replacement for Judas to be one of the twelve apostles, the essential qualification was that he must be an eyewitness (Acts 1:21, 22). At Pentecost Peter declared, "God has raised this Jesus to life, and we are all witnesses of the fact" (Acts 2:32). When Paul, because he was not one of the Twelve, had to defend his apostleship, he declared, "Am I not an apostle? Have I not seen Jesus our Lord?" (1 Cor. 9:1). The apostles were first-person witnesses because they saw, heard, and touched (1 John 1:1). That witness is foundational for the church (Eph. 2:20). The apostles are now dead, most of them having sealed their testimony with their blood, but their witness survives in the form of the New Testament.

As if the apostolic witness to the historical verity of Christ's glory were not enough, Peter appeals also to prophecy (1:19-21). Does he mean prophecies about the last days in the writings that became the New Testament (Mark 13:22; 2 Thess. 2:9; 1 John 2:18; Jude 4; and so forth), or does he mean the Old Testament prophecies? The latter meaning is more probable, for he speaks of the "prophecy of Scripture" (1:20), and the Scriptures at that time meant the Old Testament. But the other meaning is not impossible, since Peter seems to include the writings of Paul among the Scriptures (3:16). However, the reference to the morning star in 1:19 sounds like a reference to Numbers 24:17, "a star will come out of Jacob." The apostles saw the morning star as a symbol of Jesus (Rev. 22:16) and the approaching dawn as a symbol of the second coming (Rom. 13:12; Heb. 10:25).

Peter expects the morning star to rise "in your hearts" (1:19), showing the present spiritual significance of belief in the second coming of Christ. The greatest value now of the blessed hope is that it illuminates our lives today. But there is a further meaning to the words "a light shining in a dark place, until the day dawns and the morning star rises in your hearts." The prophecies have a function only *until* that which is prophesied comes, just as a candle has a function only until daylight comes. As Paul said, "Where there are prophecies, they will cease . . . but when perfection comes, the imperfect disappears" (1 Cor. 13:8, 10).

Peter may be thinking of any number of Old Testament prophecies, but the one most likely to be on his mind is that of the coming of the Son of Man and the judgment in Daniel 7:13-27, one of the most important Old Testament prophecies for the early church.

But Peter has not yet made his point against his opponents until he nails down the inspiration and reliability of the Scriptures. This he seeks to do in 1:20, 21. Unfortunately, Peter does not express himself as clearly here as we might wish, but the interpretation reflected in the NIV is most likely correct. The question is whether verse 20 says no prophecy of Scripture came about by the prophet's own interpretation, as the NIV has it, or whether it says no prophecy of Scripture is a matter of one's own interpretation, as the KJV understands it. While it is true than one's idiosyncratic personal interpretation of Scripture ought to be suspect if it diverges too radically from what has been generally understood in the history of the faith, it would be wrong for the interpretation of the Bible to be dependent on the official decision of some church hierarchy.

The fact is that anciently, people believed that revelation and interpretation of the revelation were two different processes, both needing the operation of the Holy Spirit. In the case of Nebuchadnezzar's dream, the king of Babylon received a prophetic revelation, but he could not understand what it meant until Daniel came along with the inspired explanation (Dan. 2). In that case the prophecy and the interpretation of the prophecy came to two different individuals. In other cases both the revelation and its meaning were given to the same person, either at the same time or at two different times, as in Daniel 7 and 8. First Peter 1:10-12 says that the prophets did not understand how their prophecies were going to be fulfilled; that was not known until Christ came. It is to this phenomenon that Peter is referring in 2 Peter 1:20.

The prophecies of false prophets (such as Hananiah in Jeremiah 28) were their own ideas, their own wishful thinking. But true prophecy "never had its origin in the will of man, but men spoke from God as they were carried along by the Holy Spirit" (vs. 21). This is the only mention of the Holy Spirit in 2 Peter, and the implication is that just as the Holy Spirit was needed to inspire true prophecy, even so we need the Holy Spirit's guidance to understand it and to apply it rightly to our lives and the life of the church.

It is important to note carefully how Peter understands inspiration to work. He says clearly "men spoke." That shows the human side of the Bible. It is human speech. But they spoke "from God." That shows the divine side of the Bible. It is God's message. The Bible is the Word of God in the words of men. We must not discount the divine origin of the Bible's message, even though the language, form, and style in which it comes is thoroughly human—as, in fact, we see clearly in the case of this very epistle! The writers of the Scriptures "were carried along by the Holy Spirit." The Holy Spirit did not give them their words—they used the words they had. But the Holy Spirit gave them the message and impelled them to deliver it. "The prophets raised their sails, so to speak (they were obedient and receptive), and the Holy Spirit filled them and carried their craft along in the direction he wished" (Green, cited by Hillyer, 181).

Peter has now staked out his position and set up his artillery. He is prepared to open fire with ammunition taken (and adapted) from Jude.

■ Applying the Word

2 Peter 1

1. Am I a servant of Jesus Christ? How can I know? List specific evidence that Jesus is Lord in your life.
2. Do I really know God and Jesus Christ? (See 1 John 2:3-6.) What changes might come about in my life if I knew God and His Son better?
3. Can I be sure that I am saved—that my calling and election are sure? How? To what extent does my life line up with Peter's moral imperatives as given in 1:3-11?
4. Am I growing in grace, and is my character developing the way God wants it to develop? What specific evidence can I list?
5. Do I really believe that Jesus will come in glory to welcome me into His eternal kingdom? Why?
6. Do I understand the relationship between the human and the divine aspect of the Scriptures? Explain in a few sentences your understanding of the roles of both God and prophet in revelation. How are they similar? How are they different? What single factor gives me the greatest assurance that the Bible's message is of divine origin?
7. Do I have confidence in the messages of the apostles and prophets?

■ Researching the Word

1. There is hardly any verse of Scripture that Ellen White cited more often than 2 Peter 1:4. Find the list of references in the *Seventh-day Adventist Bible Commentary*, 7:602, and look up as many of them as possible, noting how she applies the verse in each. You may also consult the *Index to the Writings of Ellen G. White*. Summarize your findings.
2. Using a concordance, make a study of the subject of the kingdom of God (and kingdom of heaven). Write a paragraph defining what it is.
3. Look up the virtue lists, the references for which are given on page 139, and compare them, if possible, by writing them in parallel columns.
4. In a good Bible dictionary, look up and read the articles "Knowledge" and "Gnostics."
5. Using a concordance, look up as many references to the Holy Spirit as you can. Make a list of the works and functions He performs.
6. Keeping in mind that different Bible versions translate them differently, make a study of the eight virtues of 2 Peter 1:5-7 by looking them up in a concordance that is based on the Bible version you use.

■ Further Study of the Word

1. For a good study of the eight virtues that Peter lists, read B. E. Seton, *Meet Pastor Peter*, 29-35.
2. For a theological discussion of the incommunicable attributes and communicable attributes of God, consult L. Berkhof, *Systematic Theology*, 57-81.
3. For a summary of the basic Gnostic myth, see B. Layton, *The Gnostic Scriptures*, 12-17. Plato's dialogue *Timaeus* can be found in *The Collected Dialogues of Plato*, edited by E. Hamilton and H. Cairns, 1151-1211, as well as in many abridged editions.

4. For a good discussion of the nature of inspiration, see E. G. White, *Selected Messages*, 1:15-23; see also her *Testimonies for the Church*, 5:747.

CHAPTER SIX

Warning Against
False Teachers

2 Peter 2:1-22

Having just spoken of true prophets in 1:19-21, Peter now deftly makes the transition to his central concern about false teachers by linking them to the false prophets of Old Testament times (2:1). He complains of their insidiousness and seductiveness, as well as of the disrepute they bring upon the church (vs. 2), but he emphasizes that judgment is coming upon them (vs. 3).

In support of the latter point, the certainty of judgment upon these brazen purveyors of loose living and vain thinking, Peter recounts examples from the past that illustrate the fact that God sooner or later brings punishment upon evildoers (vss. 4-10a). Here, as throughout the letter (with one exception), Peter never quotes Scripture directly, but rather, he refers to scriptural examples. When he paraphrases Jude (which seems to be the most likely explanation of the close parallel between 2 Peter 2 and Jude), Peter takes what he wants, leaves what he doesn't need, or adds freely. He mostly omits Jude's direct references and quotations from the Jewish religious books that are not in our biblical canon.

Turning from the examples of the past, Peter then focuses on those who pose the present danger (vss. 10b-22). He gives them no mercy, describing their transgressions in lurid terms taken largely from Jude and reaffirming that they, too, will suffer the same punishment as the evildoers of the past. Peter closes this section with the only direct scriptural quotation in the letter (Prov. 26:11, quoted in 2:22).

■ Getting Into the Word

2 Peter 2:1-22

Read the chapter through once to get the progression of the argument. Then read it again, comparing it to Jude, making note of similarities and differences. Finally, read it a third time, recording in your notebook the answers to the following questions.

1. Assuming that Peter has used Jude, what changes has he made in what Jude wrote? Why do you think he made those changes?

2. Make a list of all the transgressions and characteristics of the false teachers. Then write a paragraph describing them in your own words. Write another paragraph, telling how these teachers would probably describe themselves. Note what Peter discloses about their claims (for example, in 2:19).

3. List all the scriptural examples Peter mentions, and try to find them in the Old Testament. Indicate the Old Testament references. The marginal references in your Bible will prove helpful here.

4. How do you feel about the language Peter uses in denouncing the false teachers? Is it too harsh, or is it justified? Why?

5. What clues do you find that indicate how the false teachers were related to the church?

■ Exploring the Word

Warning Against False Teachers

In the previous chapter, Peter has spoken of the witness of the apostles who were true teachers (1:16-18) and of the true prophets (vss. 19-21). Now in chapter 2, he will discuss false prophets and false teachers. While the apostles "did not follow cleverly invented stories" (1:16), the false teachers deceive "with stories they have made up" (2:3), and "many will follow" them (vs. 2).

Satan has always tried to use false leaders, prophets, and teachers to draw God's people away from the way of righteousness. One of the most crucial and difficult tasks of a Christian is to develop the gift of discernment, for things are not always what they seem to be. The line between true and false cannot always be clearly drawn—for example, between conservative and liberal or between old and new or between majority and minority. Jesus was regarded as a dangerous liberal by the Pharisees, and Paul was similarly regarded by the Christians who opposed him (Gal. 2:4). Neither the new nor the old is automatically God's will. That is why what Peter has to say is so important.

When Peter compares the false teachers of his time to the false prophets of Old Testament times, it is a very apt comparison, because there were clear similarities. Jeremiah 23:14 declares that the false prophets "commit adultery and live a lie," supporting evildoing and reenacting Sodom and Gomorrah. According to Jeremiah 6:13-15, they practiced deceit and scoffed at the idea of God's judgment. Ezekiel 22:28 deplores how the false prophets "whitewash" evil deeds "by false visions and lying divinations." Their messages were the "delusions of their own minds" (Jer. 14:14). Deuteronomy 13:1-4 warned that even if a prophet foretells the future and performs miracles but says, "Let us follow other gods," we must not listen to him. Peter will point out that many of these characteristics of false prophets in Old Testament times were also those of the false teachers whom he and Jude attack.

Jesus had also warned against false teachers (Matt. 7:15-23) and had given a test to apply: "By their fruit you will recognize them" (vs. 20). He emphasized that even pious talk, pretended prophesying, and working of miracles were not dependable proofs of genuineness. He warned against false prophets in the last days whose deceptions will be so persuasive that "even the elect" are in danger of being misled (Matt. 24; compare vss. 11-13; Mark 13:22).

Paul was so concerned about this danger (Acts 20:29-31) that for three years he had warned the Ephesian believers about it "night and day with tears" (vs. 31). Echoing Jesus' Olivet prophecy, Paul makes a similar warning about false teachers presenting demonic teachings

(1 Timothy 4:1-5), teachers who have "a form of godliness" but deny its power (2 Tim. 3:5), teachers who will tell sinful people what they want to hear, turning them away from truth to myths (2 Tim. 4:3, 4). John warned against teachers who deny Christ's incarnation (1 John 4:1-3) and against miracle-working false prophets with demonic spirits (Rev. 16:13; 19:20; 20:10).

These words describe the Gnostic teachers who began to arise in the time of the apostles, but they also apply to teachers and movements that will arise as we approach the end of this present age. So we must give heed to what the apostles tell us, for things are not always what they seem to be.

Peter says that the false teachers smuggle in "destructive heresies" (2:1). The word *heresy* (Greek *hairesis*) was not always a derogatory term. It meant literally "a choice," and therefore one's choice of a political, philosophical, or religious party (as in the old English expression, "the Quaker persuasion"). In that sense the Jewish historian Josephus referred to the Jewish denominations of the Pharisees, Sadducees, and Essenes as "heresies" (Josephus, *Jewish War*, 2.118; *Antiquities*, 13.171, 293; *Life*, 12), and the term is used in the same way in Acts 5:17; 15:5; and 26:5. That is also the connotation of the word in Acts 24:5, 14 and 28:22, where Christianity is called a "heresy" in the sense of a "sect" (as the NIV translates it). But since parties or sects can also be divisive factions, the word could take on a negative meaning, and that is the way Paul uses it in 1 Corinthians 11:18 and in Galatians 5:20, where factionalism is one of the "works of the flesh" (vs. 19, KJV). Eventually the word came to mean false teachings, and perhaps it begins to have that meaning here in 2 Peter 2:1. The description of the heresies as "destructive" makes clear the negative meaning.

Whether the "destructive heresies" meant the factions formed by the false teachers or their teachings, one of the most distressing things about them was their "denying the sovereign Lord who bought them" (vs. 1). Is Peter remembering the time when he himself had denied his Lord (Mark 14:30, 72)? Is he remembering what Jesus had said in Matthew 10:33?

Peter does not clearly specify just how the false teachers denied their Lord, but in the light of the rest of his description, we can make an educated guess. The word he uses for *Lord* in Greek is not the usual one; from Jude 4, Peter has taken the word *despotēs*, which means an owner of slaves. Nowhere else in the New Testament is Jesus called *despotēs*, except possibly in the parallel passage in Jude 4, where the interpretation is debatable. Christians are the property of Jesus because He bought them, as Peter says. The price He paid was His blood, His life (1 Pet. 1:18, 19). The false teachers denied their Master by repudiating His ownership. This they did by their licentious conduct, returning to the slavery of sin. Furthermore, if they denied that Christ came in the flesh and really died on the cross (most Gnostics made such a denial), that would have been tantamount to saying that Jesus had not paid the price for purchasing them.

The false teachers claimed to be liberated and enlightened. For them, Jesus was the messenger from the realm of light who came to awaken them to their true natures, to help them discover their true selves. He did not come to die but to inform, to reveal the great knowledge. He was not their Master, and they were not His slaves. Rather, they had the spark of divinity in themselves, just as Jesus did. They were not bound by any commands. Such was their gospel, and it was attractive. Peter says that they denied the Master who had bought them for the highest price imaginable and therefore owned them. The result of their impudence would be "swift destruction"— the judgment, even though they also denied that a judgment would take place (2:1).

The false teachers were popular—"Many will follow their shameful ways" (vs. 2)—and their immorality and that of their followers brought "the way of truth," meaning Christianity, "into disrepute." "The way of truth," or simply "the Way," was an early self-designation of Christianity that we find in the book of Acts (9:2; 19:9, 23; 24:14, 22). The earliest Christians, who were all Jews, conceived of Christianity as first of all a way of life, for Judaism was mainly a system of behavior; and, for that matter, most of Jesus' instruction was about how to live. Later, when the gospel was planted among the Greeks, who were inclined toward philosophy and metaphysics, Christianity was thought of as a system of belief, the ultimate philosophy. Creed eclipsed deed. To the Romans, who were the great administrators of the ancient world, the important thing was the church as an organization, God's spiritual government on earth. But Peter simply calls it "the way of truth," meaning the true way.

Peter had worried about this same problem in 1 Peter 2:11, 12. Some so-called Christians, because of their unseemly conduct, had given the church a bad name. It was not that most unbelievers were such shining paragons of morality themselves, but they expected more of Christians because of the high claims that Christianity made. Not only did lawless behavior on the part of people claiming to be church members open the church to ridicule, but it confirmed unbelievers in their suspicion that Christianity was a subversive movement that threatened to destroy the fabric of society. So it was a serious matter for the false teachers to "bring the way of truth into disrepute." Historically speaking, it was this factor more than any other that forced the church to draw a line between heretical error and orthodoxy and to begin to define orthodoxy. The church had to disown those who misrepresented it. At the beginning, however, the concern was not about belief but about behavior. Only later did the labels of heresy and orthodoxy become tools for rigid thought control.

Peter charges that an important motivation of the false teachers is greed (vs. 3), as suggested also in Jude 11. Actually, the Greek word *pleonexia* can mean any kind of covetousness—for money, sex, or power (the three greatest temptations for any religious leader). Becoming a Gnostic guru with authority over an expanding circle of followers was a good way to get all of these things. These teachers were especially adept at attracting women (2 Tim. 3:6), achieving control over their minds, their purses, their hearts, and their bodies.

How did they do it? "With stories they have made up" (2:3). Another translation could be "fabricated doctrines." Women and sensitive men were distressed and depressed by a harsh and oppressive world. The false teachers claimed to give the explanation of why things were as they were and how to be liberated from it. They claimed they had the real gospel, really good news that could restore the self-image and self-worth of people who felt devalued by the system.

Such was the message supposedly contained in the Gnostic myths, a secret message imparted only to the worthy. People were more than willing to pay to become one of the worthy.

The Certainty of Judgment Upon Evildoers

The fraud and exploitation by these impostors will not go unpunished, says Peter (vs. 3b). They are headed for the judgment that they deny. Peter is drawing from Jude 4 the idea that their sentences were pronounced long ago, perhaps thinking of Old Testament prophecies or Deuteronomy 13:1-5.

The certainty of God's judgment finds its support in His judgment upon evildoers in the past, and Peter now cites three episodes as examples (2:4-10a). Two examples, the fallen angels and the cities of Sodom and Gomorrah, are taken from Jude 6, 7. Instead of Jude's first example of the rebellious Israelites in the wilderness (Jude 5), which he lists out of chronological order anyway, Peter cites Noah's flood as his second example (2:5). Another significant difference from Jude is that Peter balances two of his examples of punishment with examples of deliverance at the same time. He talks not only about the antediluvians but about Noah; not only about Sodom and Gomorrah but about Lot, of whom he says a great deal. He thus makes a double point: While punishing the wicked, God knows how to rescue the godly (vs. 9). It is interesting that this entire long passage (vss. 4-10b) is all one continuous sentence in Greek, and almost so (except verse 10) in the NIV!

The first example is angels who sinned and were cast into "hell" (vs. 4), as the NIV translates the verb *tartaroō*. There have been several interpretations of this passage. One is built upon a very ancient tradition that goes back to before New Testament times (for example, in the first book of Enoch). This tradition identified these fallen angels with the "sons of God" who had intercourse with the "daughters of men" and fathered children called Nephilim (Gen. 6:4). But this tradition has several drawbacks. In Numbers 13:33 the Nephilim are said to be giants; if Numbers is referring to the same race as Genesis 6:4, that would imply that those people somehow survived the Flood. A further problem facing this Jewish tradition is that Jesus seems to say that angels do not have sex (Matt. 22:30). While it is true that angels are called "sons of God" in Job 1:6 and 38:7, John applies the term also to human beings who are "born of God" (John 1:12, 13; 1 John 3:1, 2). So an alternative interpretation of Genesis 6:4 is that the phrase "sons of God" refers to the descendants of Seth, as contrasted with those of Cain.

If 2 Peter 2:4 is not referring to the incident in Genesis 6:4, what does it refer to? We immediately think of the primeval war in heaven described in Revelation 12:7-9, when the devil and his angels were cast down to earth. Of course, the book of Revelation had not yet been written when Jude and Peter wrote, but the tradition of a war happening in heaven was extremely ancient, a garbled form of it being found even among the cuneiform clay tablets of Mesopotamia (the *Enuma Elish* epic). Though the event probably preceded the creation of man, God could have informed Adam, Noah, Moses, and other prophets about what had happened.

Peter says that God cast the angels who sinned into Tartarus (the literal meaning of the Greek verb is "to Tartarize"). The word comes from Greek mythology, according to which there was war in heaven between the highest god Zeus and lesser gods, who were giants called Titans, led by their brother Kronos. Zeus defeated the Titans and cast them into the lowest part of the underworld, which was called Tartarus. Before New Testament times, the word *Tartarus* was adopted in the Greek translation of 1 Enoch 20:2 for the place presided over by the angel Uriel, where the spirits of the fallen "angels who were promiscuous with women" were imprisoned (1 Enoch 19). Ancient Jewish writers could not help noting the similarity between the Greek myth and what they knew of the war in heaven, so when they expressed the story in Greek, they used the Greek terms that were already available. Peter has divorced the word from its pagan origin, just as we do when we say that some young man has been wounded by Cupid, even though we do not believe in the Roman god Cupid.

Peter goes on to add that God put them "into gloomy dungeons," or, as some important manuscripts have it, "into chains of darkness" (see the NIV note). Just as in the case of Tartarus, Peter is using these terms metaphorically. If we need to answer the questions Where is Tartarus? Where are the dungeons? Where are the chains? the simplest answer is that they are here on earth, according to Revelation 12:9, 12. The earth is the prisonhouse of the devil and his angels, and he is held here until the final judgment (Rev. 20).

The second episode that Peter cites is the antediluvian world (2:5). God judged the wicked people of that world by sending the Flood, but He saved eight people, including Noah (the others being his three sons and the four wives). We have read about these people already in 1 Peter 3:20. Here in 2 Peter 2:5 he calls Noah "a preacher of righteousness." Genesis (6:9) says Noah was a righteous man but does not mention his preaching. ("Preacher of righteousness" can mean either that Noah preached righteousness or that he was a righteous preacher.) But Jewish tradition, found in the writings of Josephus and the rabbis, as well as in apocryphal books, affirms that Noah preached to the people of his generation.

Peter deals at length with the episode of Sodom and Gomorrah, his third example (2:6-8), greatly expanding what he found in Jude 7. The original account is in Genesis 19, but the incident was so impressive that it is mentioned many times throughout the Bible, in both Old and New Testaments, as an example of what happens to wicked people. But it is the experience of Lot, Abraham's nephew, whose family God rescued out of Sodom, that Peter dwells on. The picture he gives of Lot is rather complimentary. He describes him as a righteous man, extremely upset by the wickedness of his fellow townspeople (2:7, 8). That is a somewhat different picture from the one we might have gained from Genesis 19, where he is indeed hospitable and protective of his incognito angel guests—even to the point of offering his own daughters to the mob in order to deflect their lust from his guests! He had betrothed his two daughters to two men who appear no better than the rest of his neighbors (vss. 12-14). Even while being rescued, Lot was fainthearted and hesitant (vss. 18-20). His daughters got him drunk and committed incestuous acts with him (vss. 30-36). Of course, the biggest question is, Why did Lot continue to live in such a wicked community in the first place? All of this points to a man who was well-meaning but weak. But the important thing was that God "brought Lot out of the catastrophe that overthrew the cities where Lot had lived" (vs. 29). That, and the fact that Lot never approved of the evil that surrounded him, was enough to make him an illustration of the principle that "the Lord knows how to rescue godly men from trials and to hold the unrighteous for punishment until the day of judgment" (2:9, NIV note). The Greek suggests a punishment separate from and preceding judgment, probably meaning that the Flood and the incineration of Sodom and Gomorrah were first punishments or temporal judgments, while the final judgment is still in the future.

Poor, weak Lot! Perhaps it is encouraging that the Lord graciously considers him a righteous man. He was not the only person who has found himself unable, for one reason or another, to extricate himself and his family from a corrupt and degrading environment. Perhaps such people are trapped by economic necessity or family ties, or just by cords of routine and habit that bind them. In Lot's case it took the strong hands of angels to take him by the hand and drag him loose. But this much can be said of him: He never allowed his mind or heart to approve what he saw every day. We, too, live in a cultural environment where moral values are lying in decaying shreds; where evil is called good, and good, evil; where most consciences are anesthetized or dead. Yet God is willing to rescue us if we retain at least this one thing: if we do not lose our capability to be shocked and appalled by evil. If that goes, all is lost.

The story is told of an old rabbi who used to stand at the gate of his city and cry out against its sins as the citizens went in and out. At length, one of them said to him: "Old man, why do you continue to cry out against the sins of the people of the city? Do you really think you can change them?"

The rabbi replied: "I am not crying out against their sins in order to change them. I am crying out so that they will not change me!"

In 2:10 Peter brings the message of judgment home in a way that leads naturally to the next section, where he will focus on the characters of the false teachers. The threat of punishment is especially intended for "those who follow the corrupt desire of the sinful nature and despise authority" (vs. 10). The thought here was prompted by

Jude 8. The two characteristics of licentiousness and contempt for authority summarize the sins of the three negative examples, and they will be analyzed more fully in the following section. The word *authority* used in the NIV is too general and generic a translation of the Greek word *kuriotēs*, which literally means "lordship." These sinners are rebels against the divine government. Perhaps Peter is referring to the Gnostic contempt for the Creator God.

The Character and Destiny of the False Teachers

Peter now moves naturally into a development of his description of the false teachers, providing more details of their contempt for authority and their carnality.

"These men are not afraid to slander celestial beings," he says (vs. 10b), echoing Jude 8. *Celestial beings* translates *doxas*, which literally means "glories" or "glorious ones." In light of the next verse, the expression seems to refer to angels, either good or bad. Peter is not altogether clear here, but we know that Gnostics identified angels with the "principalities and powers" who were associated with the creator god in the governance of the material world, and for whom they had contempt. Peter goes on to say that "even angels . . . do not bring slanderous accusations against such beings in the presence of the Lord" (vs. 11). If it is a matter of good angels accusing or not accusing other angels, then the "celestial beings" must be evil angels—indeed, the beings whom Paul calls "principalities and powers" (Eph. 3:10; 6:12, KJV). It is not clear whether Peter is saying that the good angels are "stronger and more powerful" (2:11) than the evil angels or that they are stronger than the false teachers. Either thought would be true. Verse 12 is a denunciation based on Jude 10.

Affirming again that judgment will come (2:13), Peter goes on to describe more of the behavior of the false teachers. They "carouse in broad daylight" (vs. 13)—especially shocking, since even pagans usually waited until nightfall for their wild partying and considered daytime tippling a sign of degeneracy. Apparently these teachers even turned church potluck dinners and Communion services into drunken orgies (vs. 13b; compare Jude 12). In the early days of the church, the Communion service was part of a full meal, called the *agapē*, shared by all the church members.

The false teachers, as Peter already mentioned in 2:3, are greedy and sexually promiscuous (vs. 14). Hippolytus, an early Christian writer, reports that Simon the Magician taught his followers that sex outside of marriage is perfect love, and they said, "All earth is earth . . . it matters not where one sows the seed so long as it is sown" (quoted in Sidebottom, 87). Peter compares these false teachers to the prophet Balaam (2:15, 16; compare Jude 11), whom Moabite leaders had tried to hire to curse Israel and who later apparently was involved in seducing the Israelites into promiscuous relations with Moabite women, resulting in a plague. When Balaam was going to meet the Moabite leaders to hear their proposition, his donkey balked, and the Lord caused her to speak. The story is told in Numbers 22 to 24; see also Numbers 25 and 31:8, as well as Deuteronomy 23:4, 5.

Peter contrasts "the way of Balaam" with "the straight way" (2:15). *Straight* is still a synonym for *upright*, as when we call a person "a straight arrow" and speak of "the straight life." The straight life may seem too simple and naive for the high rollers of this world, but it is the best life. People who think about the results of a fast life of con-voluted affairs and continuous partying eventually come to a realiza-tion of how empty it is. Those who live this way wear themselves out unproductively and sooner or later come to despair; but worst of all, they make themselves unfit for heaven, food for worms. As someone has said, "The grass may be greener on the other side of the fence, but you still have to mow it." "Do not be deceived," said Paul. "God cannot be mocked. A man reaps what he sows" (Gal. 6:7).

Peter, inspired by Jude 12, 13, throws metaphoric epithets—as if they were stones—at the false teachers. They are waterless springs and storm-driven mists (2:17). Jude had said "waterless clouds." A waterless spring cannot deliver what it promises, and a storm-driven mist soon passes away. The false teachers promised liberty and ful-fillment, but their way ends in slavery to vice and emptiness. Peter continues his description of their behavior in 2:18. Appealing to the lower nature, they seduce new believers, people who had only recently come out of paganism. "They promise freedom, while they themselves are slaves of depravity—for a man is a slave to whatever has mastered him" (vs. 19). In preaching freedom, the false teachers probably appealed to Paul's message of Christian liberty and to such expressions as "The Lord is the Spirit, and where the Spirit of the Lord is, there is freedom" (2 Cor. 3:17). The Gnostics could put their own spin on such statements. But Peter reminds them of other statements of Paul, particularly ones such as this:

> What then? Shall we sin because we are not under law but under grace? By no means! Don't you know that when you offer yourselves to someone to obey him as slaves, you are slaves to the one whom you obey—whether you are slaves to sin, which leads to death, or to obedience, which leads to righteousness? . . . You have been set free from sin and have become slaves to righteousness (Rom. 6:15-18).

As John 8:34 says, "Everyone who sins is a slave to sin."

The tragedy is that these false teachers were once Christians who had been saved. They had escaped the corruption of the world by the true saving knowledge—"knowing our Lord and Savior Jesus Christ" (2:20). But they substituted the false "knowledge" of Gnosticism, thinking that the corruption of the world consisted of its materiality. Because of their indifference to the material world and contempt for their bodies, they actually "are again entangled" in the world's corruption and overcome, and "they are worse off at the end than they were at the beginning" (vs. 20). Jesus, too, had taught that a backslider can be in a worse state than if he had never been saved at all (Matt. 12:43-45).

We are learning that it takes more and more powerful antibiotics to combat viruses, which are able to mutate and develop resistance or immunity to the measures we take against them. The same is true of sin and salvation. It becomes harder and harder for someone who has known God before to return to Him, for the gospel loses some of its appeal when it loses its freshness. But there is hope, and Peter himself is a prime example of one who denied his Lord but made a wonderful comeback. Still, what Peter says in 2:21 needs to be taken very seriously. In verse 22, quoting Proverbs 26:11, Peter paints a repellent picture of these teachers who had once been godly and obedient to God's commandments but now, thinking themselves "liberated," wallow in sin like a dog in his vomit. They are like a pig after a bath, impatient to return to the mud, says Peter, quoting a well-known Gentile proverb.

■ Applying the Word

2 Peter 2

1. Do I still believe there is a difference between truth and falsehood? If so, how do I see these opposing themes at work in the church today? In society? In my life?

2. What is the difference between faith and presumption? Between faith and gullibility? Am I developing the gift of discernment so that I am able to distinguish between these extremes in my own life?

3. Do I believe that the Lord will bring judgment and destruction upon the guilty while preserving the life of the innocent? How do I relate to calamities that come into my life now? What does that tell me about my ability to trust God to save me when judgment falls on the guilty?

4. Am I subtly allowing the moral miasma of my society and culture to affect me? How? What steps can I take to avoid being affected by the moral decay of current society? How can I be in the world yet not be of the world?

5. Are my sensibilities to sin being blunted by society? If so, what can I do about it? Be specific.

6. What modern-day examples can I think of in which individuals have used religion to satisfy lust for power, money, or sex? Given the opportunity, could I be drawn into similar situations? If so, what steps can I take to avoid the temptation to exploit my spiritual influence for selfish gain? To resist such temptations?

7. Is my faith built on solid realities? To what extent am I able to look beyond pious slogans and currently popular religious

fads? In what ways am I influenced by these things?

8. As I read 2 Peter 2, what three texts do I find especially relevant to my life, church, or society? Why have I selected these texts, and why do I view them as being relevant?

■ Researching the Word

1. Using an exhaustive concordance, look up all the references in the Bible to Sodom and Gomorrah, and summarize the lesson connected with each reference.
2. Look up all the references to Balaam in the Bible, and then write his biography in a paragraph or two.
3. Look up all the references to Noah in the Bible, taking notes. What information can you find that adds to what we know about him from the Genesis account of the Flood?
4. Use a concordance to locate and study Paul's statements about freedom/liberty. Summarize in your own words what his teaching was on that subject. How does it complement what we find in 2 Peter? How does it differ? Decide who was right about Paul—the Gnostics or Peter?
5. In a good Bible dictionary, read the article on "angels." Try to decide who the "celestial beings" of 2 Peter 2:10 are.
6. Second Peter 2:21 is expressed in a literary form known as a "Tobspruch" (from the Hebrew word *tob*, "good/better," and the German word *Spruch*, "saying"; an awkward English equivalent is an "it-is-better saying"). Another example is Matthew 18:6, but such sayings are found in many places in both the Old and the New Testament. Look up the word *better* in a concordance, and make a collection of all the *Tobsprüche* (the German plural of the word) that you can find.

■ Further Study of the Word

1. For a practical exposition of 2 Peter 2, see B. E. Seton, *Meet Pastor Peter: Studies in Peter's Second Epistle*, 55-82.
2. For information about pagan versions of the war in heaven,

see the article "Kronos" in N. G. L. Hammond and H. H. Scollard, eds., *The Oxford Classical Dictionary*, 573-574, and the *Enuma Elish* epic in J. B. Pritchard, ed., *Ancient Near Eastern Texts*, 60-72.

3. In 1967 a fragmentary plaster inscription was found in Jordan at a place called Deir 'Alla, which describes the work of Balaam as diviner and seer. This heathen inscription dates back to Old Testament times (about 750 B.C.). To read more about this discovery, see the article on the Deir 'Allah inscription in D. N. Freedman, ed., *The Anchor Bible Dictionary*, 2:129, 130. If you want to dig into a scholarly study of everything that we know about Balaam from sources both inside and outside of the Bible, try M. S. Moore, *The Balaam Traditions: Their Character and Development.*

CHAPTER SEVEN

What to Do When the Lord Delays His Coming

2 Peter 3:1-18

"Dear friends" (vs. 1) marks the beginning of a new section in the letter, even though verses 2 and 3 continue the paraphrase of Jude (17, 18). Stating his intention in writing, Peter reviews what he said in 1:12-21 and leads into his next topics, the delay of Christ's second coming and the wrong and right way to relate to it. The reference to those who scoff at the apostles' teaching about end-time events (3:3-7) parallels what Peter has been saying about the false teachers in chapter 2. So, in a way, Peter is replaying his previous themes, but in a different key. He even repeats his reference to Noah's flood (vs. 6; compare 2:5), again as proof of a final judgment.

Dropping his voice a bit and again addressing his "dear friends," Peter instructs them on how to live in expectation of the advent, even if it seems to be delayed (3:8-14), emphasizing the practical consequences. Verses 8, 9 help to relate to the situation theologically, but 3:11-16 is practical, ending with a fascinating reference to the teaching of Paul, whose doctrines of grace and liberty were so badly distorted by the false teachers (vss. 15, 16).

Once again calling upon his "dear friends," the letter ends with a final warning involving one last salvo against the false teachers (vs. 17) and a beautiful benediction and doxology (vs. 18).

■ Getting Into the Word

Read through the third chapter of 2 Peter once; then review the contents of 2 Peter 1:12-21, and read the third chapter a second time. Finally, read through the whole letter from begin-

ning to end. Then address the following questions.

1. What is the relationship of 3:1, 2 to 1:12-21? What is the relationship of 3:3-7 to chapter 2?

2. According to 3:3, what motivated the scoffers, and according to 3:4, what rationale did they claim? What modern examples of this way of thinking do you see in the church? In society?

3. What three events did God's word cause, or will cause, according to 3:5-7?

4. How does Peter explain the seeming delay of the Lord's coming? Is this a satisfying explanation in your view? Why, or why not?

5. How do 3:9 and 3:15 explain each other?

6. What does Peter mean in 3:10 when he says, "The day of the Lord will come like a thief"? Using a concordance, find the other places in the New Testament where this metaphor is used. How do you reconcile this view with such passages as Matthew 24:23-28, 1 Thessalonians 4:16-18, and Revelation 1:7; which picture the second coming as a cosmic event obvious to everyone? Summarize your conclusions.

7. In the light of Revelation 20 and other references you can find using marginal references in your Bible or a concordance, when does the destruction described in 3:10, 12 occur?

8. List and examine the practical consequences of belief in the second advent and the final judgment, according to this chapter in 2 Peter.

9. What places in Paul's writings do you think 3:15, 16 refers to? What are the "things that are hard to understand" that Peter refers to? What implications do you see in the fact that Peter classes Paul's writings with "the other Scriptures"?

10. List all the places in the letter that mention the possibility of falling from grace, such as 3:17. List all the places that speak of growth in grace, such as 3:18. What do these lists indicate about God's saving grace?

■ Exploring the Word

Warning Against Scoffers

Peter draws a breath and, addressing his readers again as "dear friends," speaks in a different tone. This is already his second letter to them, he says (3:1), and the implication is that the first had been sent not long before. He is probably referring to 1 Peter, although we can't be sure. He says both letters were intended to stimulate their minds and remind them of the teachings of the prophets and of "our Lord and Savior through your apostles" (vss. 1, 2; compare Jude 17)—in other words, of the whole Bible. Already in 1:12 he had tactfully said that he merely intended to remind them of what they already knew (compare 3:17).

His readers were like most of us, tending to put their minds into neutral and to "go with the flow." The rut leads only downward until someone comes along and sounds a wake-up call. In such situations, it is not new information we need so much as to remember what we know all too well. In this case, what Peter's readers needed to remember was the words of the Old Testament prophets and the command of Jesus transmitted by the apostles who had preached to them. First Peter certainly contains many Old Testament quotations and alludes to the teachings of Jesus, so it answers to the description. The "command" (singular) in verse 2 must be the same commandment mentioned in 2:21. It is a collective term for all the moral instruction about how Christians should live, including that of the Sermon on the Mount. In the same way, Romans 7:12 referred to the Old Testament law in the singular as "the commandment," though Paul may have had the tenth commandment specifically in mind.

In 3:3 (compare Jude 18), Peter gets down to specifics. "In the last days scoffers will come," motivated by sinful desires and teaching the uniformitarian doctrine that the world always continues in a steady state, without divine intervention, without catastrophes, without end, and taunting: "Where is this 'coming' [*parousia*] he promised?" (3:4). Peter speaks in the future tense, even though such teachings were already being spread by the false teachers in the churches to whom he was writing. By this we understand that the same teachings will be current in the last days that lie ahead of us.

The expression "last days" deserves some attention. Perhaps we can distinguish a broader and a narrower meaning. According to Hebrews 1:2, the "last days" began with the first coming of Christ, and Peter believed that also (1 Pet. 1:20). There is abundant evidence in the New Testament that the apostles were convinced they were living in the last days and that the second coming of Christ was near. That faith has not been invalidated by the passage of two thousand years, for two reasons. First, Christ's first advent did inaugurate the Messianic Age, at least in its first phase—the Kingdom of Grace. Second, the lively expectation of Christ's second coming and the setting up of the Kingdom of Glory must be an incentive for godly living in every year of history, however many years that may be.

Rabbi Eliezer ben Hyrcanus, who taught toward the end of the first century A.D., once said: "Repent one day before your death." His disciples asked him, "Does one know on which day he will die?" The rabbi replied: "Then all the more reason that he repent today, lest he die tomorrow, and thus his whole life is spent in repentance." (Babylonian Talmud *Shabbath* 153a; compare Mishnah *Aboth* 2:10; see also McArthur and Johnston, 27, 28.) There is actually some evidence that Rabbi Eliezer was modifying a saying of his teacher Johanan ben Zakkai, who taught his disciples to be always ready for the coming of the Messiah. Similarly, Christians must always be ready for the coming of the Lord, whenever they may be living. Whether their probation ends at the Day of the Lord or at the day of their death, Christians need to be on their spiritual toes, with their bags packed and ready to go.

It was precisely this moral and spiritual prodding caused by belief in the soon coming of the Lord that made the "scoffers" uncomfortable, and so they mocked it. If there is no judgment, all things are permitted, and they preferred to follow "their own evil desires" (3:3).

"Ever since our fathers died," they said, "everything goes on as it has since the beginning of creation" (vs. 4). Bible students debate whether "our fathers" means the Old Testament patriarchs or the first generation of Christians, to whom the promise of the parousia was given. But the meaning of the rhetoric scarcely matters, since these scoffers even go on to say that nothing drastic has happened ever since Creation! This is a doctrine of uniformitarianism, against which Peter sets forth a doctrine of catastrophism. The scoffers purposely ignore two notable past instances of God's spectacular action, which give credibility to His future action. In each instance, He needed only to speak: (1) He created the earth by His word (Ps. 33:6); (2) He destroyed it by the water of Noah's flood. In addition, He preserves the world by His word for future fiery destruction (3:5-7). If God's word can create, it can also destroy.

At this point, a scoffer might quibble, Did not God promise Noah, "Never again will I destroy all living creatures, as I have done" (Gen. 8:21)? But the next verse says, "*As long as the earth endures*, seedtime and harvest, cold and heat, summer and winter, day and night will never cease" (emphasis supplied). The Jewish rabbis never understood the covenant with Noah to include more than a promise that there will not be another such flood. Many of them actually expected that there would be a second judgment by fire (see the references in Sidebottom, 119, 120).

We might still ask, however: When, precisely, will this destruction of heaven and earth occur? Will it be when Christ comes the second time, at the beginning of the millennium (Rev. 19:11–20:6), or at the end of the millennium (Rev. 20:7-10)? Second Thessalonians 1:7, 8 indicates that Christ's coming will be accompanied by "blazing fire." But Revelation 20:7-15 seems to point to the lake of fire and final judgment as occurring *after* the thousand years. This is surely the Gehenna of which Jesus spoke in Mark 9:43-48 and parallel passages. It is best to conclude that Peter's prophetic perspective does not clearly divide the events on both ends of the millennium but views them as a unit, called the day of judgment and destruction (3:7) and the day of the Lord (vs. 10). For sinners the distinction between the two phases of judgment makes little practical difference anyway. Whether they are burned once or twice, with the second resurrection in between, the final result is the same: they will perish.

The world is "kept" for the day of judgment and destruction of ungodly people (vs. 7). Just as the fallen angels were kept for judgment (2:4), the unrighteous are also kept for judgment (vs. 9), and darkness is kept for the false teachers (vs. 17)—the Greek word is the same in all these places. It is the word used for a prisoner being held until his sentence is carried out. It is only a time of waiting for the inevitable.

How to Prepare for the Day of the Lord

Addressing his "dear friends" in a gentler tone, Peter seeks to help them relate theologically to the seeming delay of the end (3:8, 9). He reminds them of a theological concept based on Psalm 90:4, "A thousand years in your sight are like a day that has just gone by, or like a watch in the night." If the Lord experiences the passing of time at all—the philosophers of the time would have questioned even that—how could His relationship to time be compared to the way human beings experience it? It is like comparing the way a human being and a fruit fly experience time. "Show me, O Lord, my life's end and the number of my days; let me know how fleeting is my life. You have made my days a mere handbreadth; the span of my years is as nothing before you" (Ps. 39:4, 5). Psalm 90:4 was a very helpful verse for Jewish religious thinkers of the time. It helped them, for example, to explain Genesis 2:17, where the Lord warned Adam against eating the forbidden fruit, "for in the day that you eat of it you shall die" (RSV). How is it, then, that Adam lived 930 years (Gen. 5:5)? Because in God's time, one day is a thousand years! (This explanation is in the book of Jubilees 4:30, written about 100 B.C.; other references are in Bauckham, 307.)

We puny people are impatient because our life span is so short. But God operates on a vastly different timetable, and it is good to remember that "like the stars in the vast circuit of their appointed path, God's purposes know no haste and no delay" (White, *The Desire of Ages*, 32).

So the Lord is not late or slow (3:9a; compare Hab. 2:3), "as some understand slowness." Perhaps the scoffers were saying that the Lord should have returned during the apostolic generation, and now that generation was passing off the scene, so the whole idea was a myth.

Perhaps they referred to the Lord's statement in Mark 9:1, "Some who are standing here will not taste death before they see the kingdom of God come with power." The Gospels follow this saying immediately with the account of the Transfiguration, which occurred six days later, with the clear implication that that event was in some sense a fulfillment of Jesus' words. This helps us to understand why Peter made such a point of the Transfiguration in 1:16-18. It helped to prove that what the apostles had taught about "the power and coming of our Lord Jesus Christ" was no myth (vs. 16)!

Now Peter gives another reason for the delay. God "is patient with you, not wanting anyone to perish, but everyone to come to repentance" (3:9; compare vs. 15). The doctrine of God's patience was based on Exodus 34:6, 7a: "The Lord, the Lord, the compassionate and gracious God, slow to anger, abounding in love and faithfulness, maintaining love to thousands, and forgiving wickedness, rebellion and sin." God wants to give people more time to repent. (See also Isa. 30:18; Eze. 33:11; and 1 Tim. 2:3, 4.) That includes the scoffers. In 1 Peter 3:20 Peter had pointed out that God waited patiently in the days of Noah. But the unspoken implication is that He does not wait forever, for the Flood did come (Exod. 34:7b, "He does not leave the guilty unpunished").

Peter has one more point to make against the scoffers: "The day of the Lord will come like a thief" (3:10). He is simply recalling the teaching of Jesus (Matt. 24:42-44; Luke 12:39, 40), which was passed on by all the apostles. Paul reminded the Thessalonian Christians of what they had already heard, "The day of the Lord will come like a thief in the night" (1 Thessalonians 5:2). The book of Revelation quotes the Lord to this effect twice: "I will come like a thief" (Rev. 3:3; compare 16:15). The similarity to a thief, of course, lies only in the unexpectedness of His coming! As the rabbis of the time said, "Three come unawares: Messiah, a found article, and a scorpion" (Babylonian Talmud, *Sanhedrin* 97a).

In 3:10 Peter develops the idea of destruction he mentioned in 3:7. The kind of thorough, fiery, cosmic destruction that Peter describes seems to correspond to that mentioned in Revelation 20:9-15, which follows the millennium (see White, *The Great Controversy*, 672), but we ought not to press the chronology too hard. Peter speaks of the Day of the Lord as a unit, as did the Old Testament prophets (Joel 1:15; 2:2, 11, 30, 31; Zeph. 1:15, 16; Isa. 13:6, 10), and indeed the book of Revelation (6:12, 13, 17) speaks of cosmic upheaval in connection with the time of Christ's advent. The Day of the Lord begins, then, with the second coming and includes all the events that occur until evil perishes. Jewish writings of the time (such as the Dead Sea Scrolls) also speak of fiery destruction at the end of time, and we can find something approaching the idea even among the Babylonians, the Zoroastrians, and the Stoic philosophers of the Greeks. But the real basis of the doctrine was the teaching of the Old Testament prophets (for example, Isa. 66:15, 16, 22-24, and Mal. 4:1).

Having dealt with the theological issue, in 3:11-14 Peter speaks of the practical consequences of belief in the Day of the Lord (called the day of God in verse 12). In light of this doctrine, the really important question is, "What kind of people ought you to be?" (vs. 11). The answer is to "live holy and godly lives," which in 3:14 is explained to mean making every effort "to be found spotless, blameless and at peace with him." If believing in the second advent of Christ and the judgment does not make us better people, what good is such a belief? Causing us to fear and nothing more does not suffice. It may even do more harm than good. But causing us sincerely to repent brings every good.

Verse 12a presents an intriguing translation problem, reflected in the footnote of the NIV and the RSV, as well as of other modern versions. Should it be translated "as you wait eagerly for the day of God to come," as the NIV footnote has it, or should it read "as you look forward to the day of God and speed its coming," as the NIV main text has it? Can believers really hasten that day, in spite of what Peter said in 3:8, 9? An obvious answer is that if the Lord is waiting for "everyone to come to repentance" (vs. 9), then the Day of the Lord can be hastened by repentance. The question of whether God's purpose can be hastened by human action is an old one. The Talmud records a classic debate on this subject between Rabbi Eliezer ben Hyrcanus and Rabbi Joshua ben Hananiah (Babylonian Talmud, *Sanhedrin*, 97b-98a). Rabbi Eliezer declared that the final deliverance will come if Israel repents. Rabbi Joshua replied that the time is predestined, but God will send a great persecution before the time that will cause Israel to repent. Another rabbi said, "All the predestined dates for redemption have passed, and the matter now depends on repentance and good deeds." Yet another rabbi declared, "The son of David will come only in a generation that is either altogether righteous or altogether wicked."

Like the rabbis, Christians also come face to face with a profound paradox. Ellen White, who said that "God's purposes know no haste and no delay" (*The Desire of Ages*, 32), also wrote:

> Christ is waiting with longing desire for the manifestation of Himself in His church. When the character of Christ shall be perfectly reproduced in His people, then He will come to claim them as His own.
>
> It is the privilege of every Christian not only to look for but to hasten the coming of our Lord Jesus Christ (2 Peter 3:12, margin). Were all who profess His name bearing fruit to His glory, how quickly the whole world would be sown with the seed of the gospel. Quickly the last great harvest would be ripened, and Christ would come to gather the precious grain (White, *Christ's Object Lessons*, 69).

The paradox connected with the redemption of the church and of the earth is parallel to that involved in the redemption of individuals. What does God do, and what does a person do? Does my salvation depend on God or on me? Some theologians emphasize divine sovereignty and grace; others stress human responsibility. Of course, both sides are right! Just as we require two theories to explain the behavior of light, the wave theory, and the particle theory, we often need two seemingly contradictory concepts to explain the things of God. We call such seemingly contradictory propositions "antinomies," and they are involved in all the central convictions of the Christian faith. And so, if someone asks whether salvation depends on the sovereign and irresistible will of God or on human repentance and conversion, the answer must be: Both of the above!

While God is sovereign, He takes the human response into account.

Beyond the fiery destruction of the world, says Peter, lies the promise of "a new heaven and a new earth, the home of righteousness" (3:13). The creation is moving toward a goal, and the destruction of the old world will be but a cleansing preparation for a renovated one, a world where righteousness will be at home and rule. The vision of such a renewed heaven and earth was first given to Isaiah (65:17; 66:22); this is the promise Peter refers to. In the period that led up to the New Testament, it was cherished by pious Jews whom we call apocalypticists. Finally, it was affirmed by the New Testament writers (Matt. 19:28; Rom. 8:21; Rev. 21:1, 27; and Peter).

The coming of that day is the great hope that gives aim and purpose to all existence. The alternative is cynicism and despair, as we can see in the inscriptions on Roman tombs along the Appian Way. "I was not, I became; I am not, and I care not." "Eat, drink, enjoy yourself, then join us." "While I lived, I lived well; now my little play is ended, soon shall yours be; goodbye and applaud." (These epitaphs are selected from those quoted in Angus, 104.) This desperate taking of refuge in passing pleasure is still all that many have, and we see it pathetically expressed in the autobiography of the modern agnostic, Bertrand Russell:

> What else is there to make life tolerable? We stand on the shore of an ocean, crying to the night and the emptiness; sometimes a voice answers out of the darkness. But it is the voice of one drowning; and in a moment the silence returns. The world seems to me quite dreadful; the unhappiness of many people is very great, and I often wonder how they all endure it. To know people well is to know their tragedy: it is usually the central thing about which their lives are built. And I suppose if they did not live most of the time in the things of the moment, they would not be able to go on (quoted in *Christianity Today*, 21 November 1969, 25).

Peter reminds us that the future has meaning when we place it in

God's hands, knowing that He is planning something better than what we see now.

Peter again addresses his "dear friends" as people who are looking forward to the righteous new world and tells them that this hope requires them to "make every effort to be found spotless, blameless and at peace with him" (3:14). The expression "make every effort" (*spoudasate*, "strive") is exactly the same that Peter used in 1:10. It is no passive waiting that our hope calls for. The expression "spotless and blemishless" (as the Greek literally reads) is another *hendiadys*, but it is not peculiar to 2 Peter. Peter had applied similar words to Christ in 1 Peter 1:19, and Paul applies them to the church in Ephesians 5:27. Colossians 1:22 declares that God has now reconciled us through Christ's atoning death "to present you holy in his sight, without blemish and free from accusation" if we continue in our faith. These references show that it is Christ's work that makes us spotless and blameless, but 2 Peter 3:14 says that we must also strive to be found in that state.

Perhaps we have another paradox here, but if we put all these things together, it seems to say that our effort is directed at continuing in our faith, and that continuance results in our being spotless and blameless when the day comes. The alternative to continuing in our faith is the falling that Peter has mentioned as a danger in 1:10 and 2:20. He will mention it again in 3:17. Only the blood of Christ can remove our dirty spots; only His grace can lift our blame. By faith we grasp it. By effort we maintain our faith. John 15:5-8 calls it remaining in Him and says it is the only way to bear fruit. No amount of effort can make a dead branch bear fruit, and a branch that is disconnected from the vine dies.

"Our Lord's patience means salvation" (3:15a), Peter continues, restating the point he made in 3:9. Perhaps a more precise way of stating it would have been that the Lord's patience preserves an opportunity for salvation through repentance. The delay of the day is not because of God's slowness; it is, rather, a manifestation of His patience. Peter points out that Paul's letters to them teach the same thing (vs. 15b). Actually Paul's clearest surviving statements on the subject are in his letter to the Romans, which was not written to the Christians of Asia Minor, the presumed recipients of Peter's two letters. But such teachings could have been contained in other Pauline letters that have not survived (see Col. 4:16). He did teach it in his letter to the Christians in Rome: "Do you show contempt for the riches of his kindness, tolerance and patience, not realizing that God's kindness leads you toward repentance?" (Rom. 2:4; compare 3:25; 9:22; 11:22).

But in a broader sense Paul "writes the same way in all his letters, speaking in them of these matters" (3:16). It is true that Paul never neglects to urge repentance and godly living. A common pattern in his letters is to write first of what God has done for us in Christ and then to follow that with instruction about what we are to do for Him, bearing the fruit of righteous lives. Paul, like Peter, had also warned that "the day of the Lord will come like a thief in the night" (1 Thess. 5:2).

Peter's invoking of Paul's writings in support of what he has been saying is important, because the false teachers had been claiming Paul's support for their antinomianism and libertinism. Peter acknowledges in 3:15 that Paul was given wisdom by God (that is, he was inspired by the Holy Spirit), but he admits that his letters "contain some things that are hard to understand, which ignorant and unstable people distort, as they do the other Scriptures, to their own destruction" (vs. 16). It is true that Paul ought to have been more careful about how he sometimes expressed himself—for example—in letters such as Galatians and Romans. Some of his statements were vulnerable to misinterpretation, and false teachers exploited every such possibility.

It is clear from this problem that the inspiration of the Holy Spirit did not extend to the words and expressions that the Bible writers used, but only to giving them the messages that they were to deliver. The messages were from God, but the way of expressing them was human. Failure to recognize this fact leads "ignorant and unstable people" into many fatal errors.

Summing Up and Praising

Yet again Peter addresses his "dear friends" and condenses the burden of this letter down to its very nub: "Be on your guard so that you may not be carried away by the error of lawless men and fall from your secure position" (vs. 17). The word for *secure position* could also be translated "firm footing." *Error* can also mean "deception." Deceivers are commonly themselves deceived. It can even happen that a person begins by deliberately lying and ends up sincerely believing his own lie. Say anything often enough and long enough, and you will believe it yourself. The word for *lawless* or *immoral* is the same word that was used to describe the men of Sodom in 2:7. In a word: Don't be deceived by the libertines!

On the contrary, "Grow in the grace and knowledge of our Lord and Savior Jesus Christ" (vs. 18a). These words summarize the program of growth laid down in 1:5-10 and correspond to the benediction at the beginning of the letter (1:2) and to the purpose stated at the end of Peter's earlier letter (1 Pet. 5:12). Growth is possible; growth is demanded. We need never stop growing spiritually.

The letter ends with a simple but beautiful doxology, praising the Lord Jesus (3:18b). Most of the biblical doxologies are to God the Father, but there is one other doxology lifted up to Jesus in Revelation 1:5, 6. Assuredly, such praise does not make the Father jealous of His Son. Let us live doxologically. The real test of our thoughts, doctrines, and lives is that they glorify God in Jesus Christ.

■ Applying the Word

2 Peter 3:1-18

1. What things that I already know do I need to be reminded of? What should I do about these things?
2. Has my expectation of the Day of the Lord faded or grown dim? In what ways has it affected the way I live? Be specific. Am I ready for the Lord to come? How does one become ready?
3. Can I match the Lord's patience with my patiently waiting upon Him? How does human patience differ from God's? How is it similar?
4. Am I making every effort to maintain my connection with the Lord through faith? What is my role? What is God's role?
5. Why am I looking forward to a new heaven and a new earth?

List specifics. What is the single most attractive thing to me about life in the new earth? What, if anything, makes me hesitant about life in eternity? Am I really sure I will feel at home in a world where only righteousness dwells? Why, or why not?

6. What is my concept of inspiration? How do I see the process working? How does my view harmonize with what I actually see happening in the Bible? What effect does correct interpretation of Scripture have on my relationship with Jesus?

7. Am I vulnerable to religious con artists? Why? How? What things that I am presently doing in my spiritual life can help me guard against falling through deception? What things do I need to be doing to avoid being deceived?

8. Do I live doxologically? In what ways can my life praise God?

■ Researching the Word

1. Using marginal references and a concordance, try to find all the passages in the Bible that mention the destruction at the end of time. Study these passages, and try to discover the nature of the destruction and whether it is possible to pinpoint its timing. Summarize your findings in your 2 Peter notebook.

2. Scan the letters of Paul, and make a list of the things he wrote that agree with what Peter has written. Make another list of things he said that could have been misunderstood and exploited by the false teachers.

3. With the aid of a concordance, locate as many passages as possible that mention God's patience, noting the contexts. Then write a paragraph describing what God is patient about, why He is patient, and what our response should be to His patience.

■ Further Study of the Word

1. On the general question of how to relate to the delay of Christ's second coming, see J. Paulien, *What the Bible Says About the End-Time*, and R. E. Neall, *How Long, O Lord?*

2. As noted in chapter 5, a helpful discussion of the nature of inspiration can be found in E. G. White, *Selected Messages*, 1:15-23. A thorough but somewhat controversial study is provided by A. Thompson, *Inspiration: Hard Questions, Honest Answers*.

3. The best collections of Jewish apocalyptic writings in the centuries leading up to the New Testament period are those of H. F. D. Sparks, ed., *The Apocryphal Old Testament*; and J. H. Charlesworth, ed., *The Old Testament Pseudepigrapha*, 2 vols. In these works you can find translations of such books as 1 Enoch and the book of Jubilees.

4. The people who produced the Dead Sea Scrolls also believed in fiery destruction at the end of time. See G. Vermes, *The Dead Sea Scrolls in English*, 3rd ed., where you can find an example on pages 173, 174.

PART THREE

Jude

Dangers in the Church

Introduction to
the Letter of Jude

Most commentaries on 2 Peter combine it with Jude, and many of them take up Jude before taking up 2 Peter. That is because the middle part of 2 Peter appears to be a paraphrase and adaptation of most of Jude. Certainly Jude's main concerns are also those of 2 Peter, but there are differences, and right now you should read through the twenty-five verses of Jude, comparing them to 2 Peter 2:1 to 3:3. Then read Jude again, thinking only of Jude. Now consider the following questions.

1. **What similarities and what differences do you perceive between Jude and 2 Peter?**
2. **What had Jude originally intended to write about, according to verse 3, and what did Peter write about it?**
3. **What verse in Jude states his purpose most succinctly? What is Jude's purpose, stated both positively and negatively?**
4. **Applying the don't-put-beans-up-your-nose principle, write a description of the doctrines and practices of the false teachers whom Jude warns against.**
5. **Make a list of the main ideas of the letter.**
6. **Make a list of three things Jude says that especially appeal to you as valuable for your life or for the life of the church.**

Now that you have begun to think about this little letter, let us notice some things about it.

The author says his name is Jude (the Jewish name is Judah; in Greek it is Judas), but which Jude/Judas? It was a very common Jewish name. The author says he is "a servant of Jesus Christ and a brother of James [the English form of the Jewish name Jakob]." The only Jude/Judas in the New Testament who had a brother named James was one of the Lord's brothers (Mark 6:3), presumably a half brother or stepbrother of Jesus. If Mary bore children after Jesus, James and Jude were His half brothers. But it is much more likely that they were stepbrothers, the children of Joseph by an earlier marriage, for these men treated Jesus like a younger brother. That may explain why Jude modestly refers to himself as "a servant of Jesus Christ," not "a brother of Jesus Christ," since his was not a biological relationship. James, also, though Paul calls him "the Lord's brother" (Gal. 1:19), does not refer to himself that way (James 1:1).

The relatives of Jesus (called *desposynoi* in Greek) continued to be the leaders of the Jewish church in Palestine for several generations, beginning with James. If our Jude was one of them, we may suppose that he was mainly addressing Jewish Christians in Palestine, Syria, or Asia Minor. In any case, his writing reveals a Palestinian background. Jude is immersed in popular Jewish culture and lore, though he writes in very good Greek. As we will see, he is familiar with popular Jewish literature and legends. When he refers to the Bible, though he does not quote it directly, he appears to be using the Hebrew Bible rather than the Greek translation (called the Septuagint), even though he is writing in Greek. (This is noticeable in Jude 12, 13, where he takes language from Proverbs 25:14 and Isaiah 57:20.) His way of interpreting and applying the texts, whether from our canonical Scriptures or from other sources, resembles what we find used in the Dead Sea Scrolls.

For the close parallel between Jude and the middle part of 2 Peter, see the introduction to the latter book. The great majority of scholars believe that Peter paraphrased Jude, not the other way around, for why would Jude need to put out a letter that added little to what Peter had already said? Besides, Jude exhibits a careful structure that is missing in 2 Peter; it would have been hard for Jude to construct it out of what Peter had written.

Purpose of Jude

In verse 3, Jude tells us why he wrote this letter. He wanted to urge his readers "to contend for the faith that was once for all entrusted to the saints." That was not his original purpose. He had intended to write "about the salvation we share." (When Peter undertook to expand on Jude's work, he made a point of including a discussion of this topic in 2 Peter 1:3-11.) But something happened to change Jude's plans for writing. He learned that the believers to whom he was going to write were in serious danger of being misled by false teachers. This danger was the reason he had to write what he did.

Who were these false teachers? Their heresy must have been Gnostic antinomianism (opposition to law) similar to that which Peter was combating in his second letter. We know that this way of thinking infected Christian circles—both Jewish and Gentile. Perhaps these false teachers were Naasenes/Ophites (see Introduction to 2 Peter). In fact, this kind of false teaching was widespread, finding excuse in a misapplication of Paul's preaching of free grace. Paul himself had to combat it at Corinth. Sidebottom (70, 71) lists several parallels between the people Paul denounced at Corinth and those whom Jude warns against:

	1, 2 Corinthians	Jude
Sexually immoral libertines	1 Cor. 5:1, 9; 6:12-20; 10:1	7, 8, 18
Lovers of money	2 Cor. 11:7; 12:1, 12	8, 11, 16
Loud and boastful	1 Cor. 4:7; 2 Cor 5:12; 10:12	16
Claimants of spirituality	2 Cor. 11:4	19
Perverters of Communion meal	1 Cor. 11:20-22	5

Apparently these people claimed they were led by the Spirit and therefore had no need of law or "external morality." The gospel, they declared, set them free from the law. The main difference between the people whom Jude opposed and those whom 2 Peter attacked is that Jude's opponents apparently claimed to have received visions and revelations. That is why Jude denounces them as "dreamers" (verse 8) and compares them to Balaam (vs. 11), the Canaanite prophet. But they were really after money (vs. 16). They were going around from church to church, collecting money from gullible believers who were susceptible to flattery, receptive to criticism of leaders, and open to a message that said they were free to indulge base appetites.

Structure of Jude

After beginning with a normal greeting (vss. 1, 2), Jude states his purpose, which was to urge his readers to guard the faith (vs. 3). He then states the reason why this was necessary: subversion by immoral teachers (vs. 4).

The next fifteen verses (vss. 5-19) are a vigorous attack against the false teachers, which is neatly structured around four authoritative "texts" that he expounds in a midrashic fashion (Bauckham, 5, 6; D. N. Freedman, ed., *Anchor Bible Dictionary*, 3:1098). A midrash was a type of Jewish commentary that sought to bring out the underlying edifying meaning of the text. In each of these four cases, Jude alludes to groups of Old Testament types (or examples) or quotes a prophecy found outside the Old Testament. He then applies the type or the prophecy to the false teachers. The Old Testament types are in two groups of three—rebellious Israelites, fallen angels, Sodom and Gomorrah (vss. 5-7, 11) and Cain, Balaam, and Korah (vs. 11). Their interpretations include secondary allusions to Scripture or Jewish tradition. The two quotations found in verses 14, 15 and 17, 18 are from the book of Enoch (a work that was popular among Jews and Christians but unworthy of being included in the biblical canon) and from apostolic teaching respectively.

In verses 20 to 23 Jude returns to his positive purpose, exhorting the readers to guard and contend for the faith. The letter concludes with a beautiful doxology (vss. 24, 25).

This analysis yields the following outline:

For our purposes it will be convenient to deal with Jude in two chapters, keeping all denunciations of the false teachers together in the first and beginning the second with verse 20.

The Problem of Apocryphal Quotations and Allusions

Jude 14, 15 directly quotes from a book that circulated widely in New Testament times among both Jews and Christians. It is now called 1 Enoch, because a good deal of "Enoch" literature was produced, and we know of at least two other books bearing his name. All of these books purport to be the words of Enoch, the antediluvian saint about whom we read in Genesis 5:24. Enoch was a fascinating figure because God took him to heaven, apparently without seeing death. Pious Jews figured that Enoch's special status in heaven gave him unique insights. The possibility, however, that any of the so-called books of Enoch contain anything actually written by the Enoch of Genesis, "the seventh from Adam," is so remote that we can safely say that it is impossible. This conclusion will be obvious to anyone who takes the trouble to read these books.

First Enoch is also called Ethiopic Enoch, because for a long time the only known complete copies were in the Ethiopic language. A few pages in Greek were also known. The book is part of the biblical canon accepted by the Ethiopian Coptic Church. When the Dead Sea Scrolls were discovered, the situation changed dramatically. Recovery of the ancient scrolls from the caves beside the Dead Sea brought to light several large sections of 1 Enoch in its original Aramaic language. Intense study has shown that 1 Enoch is made up of five parts that were originally separate. The first part is the oldest, probably having been written in the third century B.C. It is from this part that Jude's quotation comes.

First Enoch is said to be pseudepigraphical, because it is attributed to a famous person who did not really write it. Many such pseudepigrapha were produced in the centuries just before New Testament times. First Enoch is also called an apocalypse, because it purports to reveal cosmic realities and future realities. The first part, consisting of thirty-six chapters, is called the Book of the Watchers. It tells about the fall of the disobedient angels and the judgment that is to come. No doubt Jude's quotation was taken from the Greek version or the original Aramaic, but the Ethiopic version of 1 Enoch 1:9 reads as follows in English:

> And behold! He comes with ten thousand holy ones to execute judgment upon them, and to destroy the impious, and to contend with all flesh concerning everything which the sinners and the impious have done and wrought against him (translation in Sparks, 185).

Besides the direct quotation, Jude refers to other stories narrated in 1 Enoch. Jude 6 refers to things we read about in 1 Enoch 10 and 12. The last part of Jude 12 and verse 13 appear to be based on

1 Enoch 2:1 to 5:4. Not only that, but Jude 9 and 16 make use of another work not found in our Bible, *The Assumption of Moses*, sometimes called *The Testament of Moses*.

Some readers find these facts troubling. How could an inspired writer use sources that we do not accept as inspired? First of all, we need to remember that Jude was not unique in this regard. The apostle Paul, when it suited his purpose, did not hesitate to quote even from pagan authors. Twice he quoted from a stanza by the poet Epimenides, which chided the people of Crete for claiming to have the tomb of the god Zeus on their island:

> They fashioned a tomb for thee, O holy and high one—
> The Cretans, always liars, evil beasts, idle bellies!
> But thou art not dead; thou livest and abidest for ever;
> For in thee we live and move and have our being
> (Horn, et. al., *SDA Bible Dictionary*, 892).

Paul cited part of this verse in his speech on Mars Hill (Acts 17:28), because the Athenians considered their poets as authoritative support for a statement. In Titus 1:12 Paul quotes another part of the verse, referring to Epimenides as "even one of their own prophets."

On Mars Hill Paul quoted from another Greek poet, Aratus, in Acts 17:28. The first five lines of Aratus's poem *Phaenomena* read:

> From Zeus let us begin; him do we mortals never leave
>   unnamed;
> Full of Zeus are all the streets and all the market-places
>   of men;
> Full is the sea and the heavens thereof;
> Always we all have need of Zeus;
> For we are also his offspring
> (Horn, et. al., *SDA Bible Dictionary*, 892).

Finally, we might notice that Paul quotes a line from a popular Greek playwright, Menander, in 1 Corinthians 15:33.

A careful search of the whole Bible for such quotations and allusions would turn up many more examples. It is simply a matter of the process of communication. Whether preacher or prophet, a communicator must use language his audience will understand, illustrations that will illuminate, and citations that will persuade. A quotation or allusion need not have the authority of canonicity to carry weight with a particular audience, but it must make contact with their hearts or their minds. When I travel abroad and have the opportunity to speak to people of a different culture, or even a different religion from my own, I try whenever possible to find some gem from their own treasury that I can use. It breaks down the barrier between us and helps communication. Today, we might cite a scientific finding when commending our faith to a scientifically minded generation. ("Studies have shown that prayer lowers blood pressure.") Anciently, a Christian communicator might refer to a poet, a philosopher, a legend, or a tradition.

But did Jude himself believe that the "Enoch" he was quoting was really "the seventh from Adam"? We will probably never know for sure. But if he did, it simply shows that he participated fully in his culture and its lore. It becomes, then, an aspect of the incarnational nature of God's revelation and inspiration. That is to say, the Bible, like Christ, is a union of the divine with the human. The message is of God, but the messengers are people of their own time and place.

Major Themes in Jude

The principal themes of this little letter flow out of its purpose and occasion, as stated in verses 3 and 4.

1. The *faith* is the underlying theme of the letter (vss. 3, 20). In Jude, faith does not mean the *act* of believing but the *object* of believing. This faith is not a formal creed; it is the gospel message.

2. Final *judgment* and doom are pronounced upon the false teachers and all unrepentant evildoers (vss. 6, 7, 13, 15, 23). Their punishment is described as fire (vss. 7, 23) and "blackest darkness" (vs. 13).

3. Jude emphasizes the polluting *evil influence* of the false teachers (vss. 12, 23). They *pervert* good things such as the message of grace (vs. 4) and the *agapē*-meal (vs. 12).

4. At the same time, Jude has a *concern for souls*, even the false teachers (vss. 22, 23).

5. Jude recognizes the possibility that *God's people may sin and fall from grace* (vs. 5), but the Lord is able to keep us from that (vs. 24).

6. Jude assumes the *Lordship and deity of Christ* (vss. 4, 17, 21, 25).

7. Jude believes in *angels*, both celestial and fallen (vss. 6, 8, 9).

8. Important to Jude's argument is a belief in *prophecy* and the prophetic or exemplary import of Old Testament types and events (vss. 7, 14, 17).

9. The *doxology* (vss. 24, 25) simply capsulizes the fundamental aim of the whole letter—that the church and its members by their lives may glorify God. The blemish of sin and licentiousness makes them unfit to do that (24, 12).

10. *Prayer* must be in the *Holy Spirit* (20), and not everyone who claims to have the Spirit really does (19).

11. The *parousia* (appearing) of Jesus Christ means doom for the sinners, but it is the hope of eternal life for sincere believers who live in expectation of it (21, 14, 24).

For Further Reading

Most of the materials suggested for the study of 2 Peter are also relevant for the study of Jude.

1. The most thorough treatment of Jude's structure and related issues are by R. J. Bauckham, in two places: Bauckham, *Jude, 2 Peter*, 3-17; and in D. N. Freedman, ed., *The Anchor Bible Dictionary*, 3:1098-1103.

2. For a thorough but somewhat technical study of the problem of pseudepigrapha in New Testament times, see D. G. Meade, *Pseudonymity and Canon: An Investigation Into the Relationship of Authorship and Authority in Jewish and Earliest Christian Tradition*. Meade has a discussion of the Enoch tradition on 91-102.

3. The most recent English translations of 1 Enoch are in H. F. D. Sparks, ed., *The Apocryphal Old Testament*, 169-319, and James H. Charlesworth, ed., *The Old Testament Pseudepigrapha*, 1:5-100.

CHAPTER EIGHT

Warnings to the People Who Have Been Called

Jude 1-19

Jude begins in the usual way for a Jewish letter (vss. 1, 2). The opening has three parts: identification of the sender, identification of the addressees, and a greeting, which is also a blessing.

That out of the way, Jude states the purpose of the letter, which is to encourage the readers to contend for the faith (vs. 3). He then discloses the reason why that encouragement is necessary—the nefarious activities of false teachers, whom he denounces (vs. 4).

This denunciation of the false teachers is developed at length in verses 3 to 19. As described in the Introduction, Jude gives us here a carefully crafted composition, a fourfold midrash (Jewish edifying commentary) in which he applies four typological or prophetic "texts" to the false teachers, showing how they are headed for a well-deserved doom.

One interesting literary feature of this section (pointed out by Hillyer, 19) is Jude's habit of using "threesomes": the readers are called, loved, and kept (vs. 1); he wishes for them mercy, peace, and love (vs. 2); he addresses them as "dear friends" three times (vss. 3, 17, 20); the false teachers are godless, immoral, and deniers of Christ (vs. 4); one trio of types is Israel, fallen angels, and Sodom and Gomorrah (vss. 5-7); "these dreamers" pollute themselves, reject authority, and slander celestial beings (vs. 8); another trio of examples is Cain, Balaam, and Korah (vs. 11); the false teachers are blemishes, brazen, and selfish (vs. 12); they cause divisions, follow carnal instincts, and do not have the Spirit (vs. 19).

■ Getting Into the Word

Jude 1-19

Read again the whole letter, and then concentrate on verses 1 to 19, answering the following questions.

1. What is the relationship of verse 3 to verses 20-23? What is the relationship of verse 4 to verses 5-19?
2. According to verse 3, what had Jude originally intended to write about but did not? If he had written about that topic, what do you think he would have said? Do you think he would have said the same thing as Peter in 2 Peter 1:3-11? Why, or why not?
3. Using the marginal references in your Bible, find out what you can about the three groups mentioned in verses 5 to 7 and about the three individuals mentioned in verse 11.
4. Make a list of the evil characteristics of the false teachers and their tactics. Make another list of the things that will happen to them.
5. Using a concordance, find all the places in the Bible that mention Enoch; then write a paragraph describing what we know about him from the Scriptures.
6. Where in the New Testament do we find apostles saying something like the prophecy quoted in Jude 18? Marginal references in your Bible will help you find the passages.
7. What clues can you find that give a picture of life in the churches this letter was sent to?

■ Exploring the Word

Greetings

In the first verse, the writer identifies himself clearly as Jude (Greek *Ioudas*, Judas). He is a brother of James (*Iakōb*). The only Judas in the New Testament with a brother by that name was the Judas who was one of the brothers of Jesus (Mark 6:3). Presumably, these men were

Jesus' older stepbrothers, and since James is mentioned first in Mark's list, Jude was probably younger. If this James is the author of the letter by that name, and if our Jude was his brother, it is noteworthy that both of them choose to call themselves servants of Jesus Christ (see James 1:1), not brothers of Jesus Christ.

Jude does not identify his addressees by personal or geographical names, but rather as "those who have been called, who are loved by God the Father and kept by Jesus Christ." Apparently this letter was really an encyclical or general letter, prepared to be sent to any and all churches that needed it. "Those who have been called" is an expression meaning "Christians." Paul also was fond of that designation (e.g., Rom. 1:6, 7), Peter preferred "chosen" (1 Pet. 1:1, 2), and the book of Revelation used both (Rev. 17:14).

The next phrase is literally "beloved *in* God the Father," which has puzzled interpreters. Perhaps the key is in 1 John 4:16, "God is love. Whoever lives in love lives in God, and God in him." Jude approaches that way of speaking in verse 21, "Keep yourselves in God's love."

The third phrase applied to the addressees is "kept by Jesus Christ," but the NIV footnote shows that here, also, it is uncertain what preposition to use. It could be "kept *for* Jesus Christ," but that seems less likely. Probably the meaning is unpacked in verse 24—Jesus Christ "is able to keep you from falling." That is reassuring, because later Jude is going to show that it is, in fact, possible to fall.

The blessings Jude prays for his readers to receive are mercy, peace, and love (vs. 2). The expression in Paul's pastoral epistles is grace, mercy, and peace (1 Tim. 1:2; 2 Tim. 1:2; see also 2 John 3). Perhaps Jude substituted *love* for *grace* because he was disturbed by the false teachers' abuse and distortion of the doctrine of grace (vs. 4). The expression "be yours in abundance" or "be multiplied" in this connection is Jewish (see Dan. 4:1 and 1 Pet. 1:2).

Jude's Purpose and Reason

Addressing his readers in a pastoral way as "dear friends," Jude now gets right to the point, but it is a different point than he originally intended (vs. 3). He had planned to compose a nice essay dealing with "the salvation we share" (or "our common salvation"), but news of danger to the church forced a change in plans. Jude's expression about salvation shared in common may have suggested the odd expression in 2 Peter 1:1, translated "a faith as precious as ours" (literally, "faith of equal value to ours"). In any case, Jude did not stop to write about the shared salvation, but Peter did (2 Pet. 1:3-11).

What Jude had to write about immediately was the need to "contend for the faith that was once for all entrusted to the saints" (vs. 3). The word for *contend* means "to struggle strenuously" and also implies confrontation, as in a wrestling match. Just how his readers were supposed to carry on the struggle will be spelled out in verses 20 to 23.

The fight is for "the faith." In Jude, faith does not mean the *act* of believing, but rather that which is believed. Some commentators think Jude is talking about a formal creed, which would suggest a late date for the letter. But such an understanding is unnecessary. In the New Testament, the word is often used to mean the gospel message. It was reported of Paul, "The man who formerly persecuted us is now preaching the faith he once tried to destroy" (Gal. 1:23). "Having faith" is trusting, but "preaching the faith" means proclaiming a message with a certain content. Again, Acts 6:7 speaks of becoming "obedient to the faith." In such places, the word is being used the same way Jude uses it.

This faith "was once for all entrusted to the saints" (vs. 3). *Saints* is another word for *Christians*. It is not used of individuals in the New Testament, but rather in the plural, collectively, for the corporate body of Christians, the church. Christians are holy as a body, in relationship with each other. After New Testament times, some Christians thought the only way to be holy was to withdraw from society and live solitary lives (for example, "Saint" Anthony). If they succeeded in achieving sainthood, they would have no way of knowing it, for sanctity is tested by trying to relate to difficult people! That is one reason why we can be saints only in groups.

The Christians to whom Jude was writing had the gospel message delivered to them (1 Cor. 15:1) "once for all" (vs. 3). Jude says this to warn against any revision of the message, any deviation from the

original preaching and teaching that they heard when they first became Christians. The idea is similar to Paul's in Galatians 1:9, "If
anybody is preaching to you a gospel other than what you accepted,
let him be eternally condemned!" It is going to become clear that
Jude was worrying about a gutted gospel that had been stripped of its
moral implications, not about a system of metaphysical propositions.

Why was it necessary to struggle in behalf of a morally relevant faith?
Jude gives the reason in verse 4. "Certain men" are deviously teaching
otherwise. These are not ordinary believers, but teachers, for they are
leading others astray, not just erring by themselves. They were infiltrat-
ing the churches by stealth, not like honest, straightforward men.

Jude describes them as impious, irreverent—the NIV uses the word
godless, but the word does not necessarily mean an atheist. These
teachers did not deny the existence of God, but they did not respect
Him. If they were typical Gnostics, they believed that the Creator of
this world is a stupid blunderer. "In Your face, God!" was their attitude.

Jude tells us that these teachers "change the grace of our God into
a license for immorality." It was typical of many Gnostic groups that
they used the gospel message of grace—especially as Paul expressed
it—as a pretext for throwing out the law of God, in fact, all law. "We
walk not by law but by the Spirit," they claimed; "we are through
with externals like the commandments; we are liberated." In Romans, Paul sought to correct such gross misunderstandings (Rom.
3:8; 6:1, 15; compare Gal. 5:13).

Even worse, Jude says these teachers "deny Jesus Christ our only
Sovereign and Lord" (vs. 4). The word *sovereign* (Greek *despotēs*) is
used of Jesus elsewhere only in 2 Peter 2:1. Here, the phrase reads
literally "denying the only Master and our Lord Jesus Christ," and it
is not certain whether "Master/Sovereign" refers to God the Father
or whether both titles, Master and Lord, apply to Jesus Christ. Peter
certainly applies it to Jesus, and that suggests a similar meaning in
Jude, even though there are no other parallels to this usage in the
New Testament—all the other places where *despotēs* is used apply the
title to God the Father. Another clue that early Christians applied it
to Jesus is the fact that they called Jesus' relatives *desposynoi*, a word

derived from *despotēs*. This rather technical debate is important, because it shows us that Christians very early regarded Jesus as God, coequal with the Father.

But how did the false teachers deny their Master and Lord? It is true that classical Gnosticism denied the unique sovereignty of God doctrinally, by distinguishing between the Most High God and the demiurge creator god. (For a discussion of Gnosticism, see the Introduction to the Second Letter of Peter.) It also denied Christ doctrinally by denying the Incarnation (1 John 2:22, 23). But the rest of Jude's letter suggests that he is thinking of something else. The false teachers denied the Lord by their behavior. Titus 1:16 speaks of this kind of denial: "They claim to know God, but by their actions they deny him." Jesus had said, "Not everyone who says to me, 'Lord, Lord,' will enter the kingdom of heaven, but only he who does the will of my Father who is in heaven" (Matt. 7:21).

Jude tells us that the doom of the false teachers was prophesied. Their "condemnation was written about long ago" (vs. 4). The verb can also mean "prescribed," "proscribed," or "designated," but the NIV translation fits well with the section that follows, which is a series of types (examples) and prophecies shown to apply to the false teachers. What comes next, then, unpacks Jude 4.

The Degeneracy and Doom of the False Teachers

As Peter did (2 Pet. 1:12), Jude tactfully presents his warning as a reminder of something his readers already knew (vs. 5). He begins with the example of three groups of evildoers in biblical history: the rebellious Israelites in the Exodus, the fallen angels, and Sodom and Gomorrah (vss. 5-7).

The people of Israel were the people of God, and God delivered them from the bondage of Egypt. Yet they rebelled in the wilderness (Num. 14), and the rebels did not enter the Promised Land (Num. 26:64, 65). They were lost (1 Cor. 10:5). Jude reminds his readers of these facts as a warning that even though they are Christians saved by grace, they can be lost if they rebel and fall. "The Lord delivered his people out of Egypt, but later destroyed those who did not believe" (vs. 5). Saved but then lost! (Second Peter 1:10, 2:20, and 3:17 warn against the same dreadful possibility.)

The second group in Jude's first trio of examples is the fallen angels (vs. 6), a symbol that was also picked up and developed in 2 Peter 2:4. First Enoch, a book that Jude obviously knew, identified the fallen angels (the Watchers) with the "sons of God" who, according to Genesis 6:1, 4, had sexual relations with "the daughters of men." (See 1 Enoch 6–19; 22:11; etc.) For the theological difficulties in this interpretation, see the comments on 2 Peter 2:4. It may be that Jude is not thinking here of a biblical incident, but of the conflict in heaven that is alluded to in such places as Isaiah 14:12-15; 24:21, 22. Jude does not mention that the angels committed sexual transgressions, even though the false teachers did. He says that they "did not keep their positions of authority" (vs. 6). Apparently they were not satisfied with their status. As a result, they are kept in the darkness of the earth, a darkness of their own making, waiting for the judgment ("the great Day," an expression found in 1 Enoch). The implication is that the false teachers face the same destiny.

The third group held up as an example is the people of Sodom and Gomorrah and environs (vs. 7), which 2 Peter 2:6-10 develops at length. In this case, as Jude makes clear, the sin is definitely sexual immorality and perversion. Because their cities were destroyed by fire (Gen. 19:24), "they serve as an example of those who suffer the punishment of eternal fire." The NIV translation of this verse is inferior to others. For example, the NRSV says that they "serve as an example by undergoing a punishment of eternal fire." The fire that destroyed Sodom and Gomorrah was eternal in the sense that its result was irreversible. It is interesting, however, that Jude's contemporaries thought the fire was still smoldering and visible south of the Dead Sea! The apocryphal book Wisdom of Solomon says, "Evidence of their wickedness still remains: a continually smoking wasteland, plants bearing fruit that does not ripen, and a pillar of salt standing as a monument to an unbelieving soul" (10:7, RSV). The Jewish historian Josephus writes, "There are still the remainders of that divine fire; and the traces of the five cities are still to be seen, as well as the ashes growing in their fruits, which fruits have a color as if they were fit to be eaten; but if you pluck them with your hands, they will dissolve into smoke and ashes" (*Jewish Wars*, 4.484). The ancients regarded what they believed to be the smoking remains of the cities of the plain as an ever-present, "eternal" reminder of the results of sin and a visible symbol of future judgment (Deut. 29:23; Jer. 49:17, 18). Such a judgment is awaiting the false teachers.

Like those in the three fearful examples Jude has placed before them, the false teachers have committed similar crimes (vs. 8). He refers to them as "these dreamers," suggesting that they claimed to have received visions (compare Joel 2:28, 29 and Acts 2:17). But whatever their claims, or because of their claims, they "pollute their own bodies" like the Sodomites, they "reject authority" like the rebellious Israelites, and they "slander celestial beings" like the fallen angels.

This bill of charges sums up their iniquity. Some early Gnostics (see Introduction to 2 Peter) called sexual promiscuity "perfect love" and organized ritual orgies. They all rejected the authority of the Creator God. The meaning of the third charge is more obscure. The "celestial beings" (NIV) translates a word that literally means "glories," a term in the Dead Sea Scrolls used for angels. The parallel passage in 2 Peter 2:10b is equally difficult, though there the meaning might be evil angels. That may not be Jude's meaning. The Gnostics taught that associated with the demiurge were celestial beings (*archōntes*) who served as jailers of the human spirit. If they can be identified with angels, that could be Jude's idea here. On the other hand, if he intends an analogy between verse 8 and verse 9, then the "celestial beings" are parallel with the devil in verse 9, which would make them evil angels, at least in the opinion of the false teachers, as may be the case in 2 Peter 2:10b. We cannot now be sure just exactly what Jude (and 2 Peter) meant, but his estimation of the angels was probably quite different from that of the false teachers.

Jude 9 contrasts the attitude of the archangel Michael with the attitude toward the angels exhibited by the false teachers. The point seems to be that it is presumptuous to bring a complaint against heavenly beings, for whatever reason, for God alone has authority to pass judgment upon them. Even Michael, in arguing a just cause against the devil, did not presume to pass judgment, rather deferring the matter to the Supreme Judge.

Who is Michael? A heavenly messenger told Daniel that Michael is "one of the chief princes," the only one strong enough to help him against "the prince of Persia" (Dan. 10:13, 20, 21). Daniel 12:1 describes him as "the great prince" who protects the people of God and who will arise to deliver them in the final time of trouble. He is the defender and advocate of God's people, no doubt the same personage as "the angel of the Lord" who defends Joshua the high priest in Zechariah 3:1-10. Astonishingly, in Zechariah 3:2 this angel is called the Lord, and he says to Satan, the accuser, "The Lord rebuke you, Satan! The Lord, who has chosen Jerusalem, rebuke you!" To Joshua, he says, "See, I have taken away your sin, and I will put rich garments on you" (3:4). In 1 Enoch, Michael seems to be the leader of the four or seven "angels of the Presence" (1 Enoch 40; 20:7). It is no wonder that the early Christian visionary and writer Hermas identified Michael with Christ, the Son of God.

But Jude is apparently citing the climactic ending of another apocryphal work that circulated in his day, containing a number of Jewish legends. That work, called *The Assumption of Moses* or *The Testament of Moses*, still mostly survives, but the ending has disappeared. It can be reconstructed, however, from several references to it in early Christian literature (see Bauckham, *Jude, 2 Peter*, 65-76). Bauckham reconstructs it as follows:

> Joshua accompanied Moses up Mount Nebo, where God showed Moses the land of promise. Moses then sent Joshua back, saying, "Go down to the people and tell them that Moses is dead." When Joshua had gone down to the people, Moses died. God sent the archangel Michael to remove the body of Moses to another place and to bury it there, but Samma'el, the devil, opposed him, disputing Moses' right to honorable burial. . . . Michael and the devil engaged in a dispute over the body. The devil slandered Moses, charging him with murder, because he slew the Egyptian and hid his body in the sand. But Michael, not tolerating the slander against Moses, said, "May the Lord

rebuke you, devil!" At that the devil took flight, and Michael removed the body to the place commanded by God. Thus no one saw the burial-place of Moses (Freedman, ed., *Anchor Bible Dictionary*, 3:1099).

But though even Michael, in defending the just cause of Joshua the high priest and the body of Moses, did not presume to accuse Satan, rather leaving that responsibility to the Ancient of Days, the false teachers did not hesitate to accuse and condemn the angels because of their rule of law.

Apparently these teachers claimed to have special knowledge about the invisible powers of the universe, a knowledge that qualified them to make judgments about them. Jude says "these men speak abusively against whatever they do not understand" (vs. 10). But far from understanding spiritual realities, they operated only on an animal level, driven only by physical appetites and passions, ungoverned by reason. It would result in their destruction, Jude predicted. Jude's words are similar to what Paul says about the enemies of the cross of Christ: "Their destiny is destruction, their god is their stomach, and their glory is in their shame. Their mind is on earthly things" (Phil. 3:19).

Pronouncing a woe upon them, Jude now moves to his second trio of examples. This time his examples are individuals: Cain, Balaam, and Korah (vs. 11). Jude 11 to 13 is not just about sinning, but about leading others into sin.

Cain was the first murderer, who slew his righteous younger brother Abel (Gen. 4:1-16). In much Jewish tradition, Cain was the prototypical sinner, the fountain of iniquity that corrupted humanity (see Wisdom of Solomon 10:3, 4; Josephus, *Antiquities* 1.52-66; other references in Bauckham, see 79, 80).

Balaam, the Canaanite prophet, was a "hired gun," a prophet for profit (Num. 22–24). Balaam devised the Moabite plot to entice Israelite men into involvement with Moabite and Midianite women and idolatry, turning them away from the Lord, resulting in a plague (Num. 25:1-3; 31:16). For this, Balaam died by the sword (Num. 31:8).

Korah the Levite led a rebellion against Moses, which was a rebellion against God (Num. 16). The Lord punished Korah and his followers by causing the earth to split apart and swallow them.

What these three individuals had in common was that they led others into sin and thus were doomed. So it was, also, with the false teachers.

Jude opens a window on early church life at the same time that he complains, "These men are blemishes at your love feasts, eating with you without the slightest qualm" (vs. 12). In early Christian practice, the Lord's Supper (like Passover) was celebrated as part of a full meal, sort of a church supper. It was called the *agapē* meal (*agapē* means "love"). Table fellowship was an important expression of mutual acceptance and unity (Acts 2:42, 46). But the false teachers were turning these occasions into drunken parties, if not orgies. Something like this happened at Corinth (see 1 Cor. 10, 11). Paul complained, "When you come together, it is not the Lord's Supper you eat, for as you eat, each of you goes ahead without waiting for anybody else. One remains hungry, another gets drunk" (1 Cor. 11:20, 21). It was probably because of abuses like this that the custom of the *agapē* feast fell out of favor.

The second part of verse 12 and all of verse 13 consist of a series of metaphors taken from Proverbs 25:14; Isaiah 57:20; and 1 Enoch. None of them are complimentary! Together, they present a picture of emptiness, vanity, barrenness, and instability. "Twice dead" (vs. 12) may be an allusion to the second death (Rev. 20:14). The "wandering stars" (*asteres planētai*) at the end of verse 13 are the planets; in fact, our English word comes from the Greek word for *wanderer*. The Greek verb *planaō* also means "to lead astray, to deceive." So there is a meaningful play on words in verse 13. The New Testament frequently warns against false prophets of the last days who will lead many astray (Matt. 24:4, 5, 11, 24; 1 Tim. 4:1; 2 Tim. 3:13; 1 John 4:6; Rev. 2:20; 13:14). Planets do not shine by their own light but only by reflected light. These "wandering stars" will be consigned to darkness forever ("outer darkness," Matt. 8:12, KJV). In contrast, Daniel 12:3 says teachers of truth will shine like the stars forever.

In the Introduction to Jude, we have already discussed the use of a direct quotation from 1 Enoch 1:9 in Jude 14, 15. It makes the third "text" that Jude applies to the false teachers. The number "seventh from Adam" is based on inclusive reckoning. The seven include both Adam and Enoch (Gen. 5:3-18). The thousands and thousands of holy ones (vs. 14) are angels (compare Dan. 4:13; 8:13). When the Lord came from Sinai, they were with Him (Deut. 33:2). When He comes again, they will be with Him (Zech. 14:5). This is emphasized in the New Testament (Matt. 16:27; 25:31 and parallel passages; 2 Thess. 1:7). He will come to judge ungodly people, ungodly deeds, ungodly methods, and ungodly words (vs. 15).

Jude 16 describes some further characteristics of these cynical teachers: they are "grumblers and faultfinders" like the rebels in the wilderness (Exod. 15:24; 17:3; Num. 14:29; etc.). This is the only place in the New Testament where these two terms are used. The false teachers are also self-serving, they talk big in order to impress others, and they win people over by flattery. The Gnostics especially went after wealthy people, skillfully playing upon their egos, their hopes and fears. These are techniques used in every age by people who are hungry for power.

The fourth and final "text" that Jude applies to the false teachers is a prophecy that the apostles made when they first preached the gospel and taught these believers. Jude merely asks them to remember it (vs. 17). "In the last times there will be scoffers who will follow their own ungodly desires" (vs. 18). This indeed was a prediction of more than one apostle, but our records of it come mostly from Paul (see Acts 20:29-31; 1 Tim. 4:1, 2; 2 Tim. 3:1-9). Similar warnings in different words are found throughout the New Testament (e.g., 1 John 4:1), and the thought really goes back to Christ's Olivet discourse (e.g., Matt. 24:11; cf. Matt. 7:15). Of course, 2 Peter 3:3-7 develops this idea.

The scoffing false teachers create divisions in the church (vs. 19). They claim to be superspiritual, but, in fact, they are carnal and worldly. Perhaps they seized upon 1 Corinthians 2:13-15, asserting that if someone did not understand or accept their incoherent babblings, it was because he was not spiritual. Jude says: Don't listen to their words until you look at their lives (vs. 19)! Jesus has given us a test: "By their fruit you will recognize them" (Matt. 7:16, 20). Don't just go by pious talk (vs. 21). A person can excel at religious talk but have no scruples. Some people are not what they seem to be.

■ Applying the Word

Jude 1-19

1. What elements in my religious experience might make me vulnerable to smooth-talking religious charlatans? What can I do to develop spiritual discernment?

2. Am I conscientious about what I teach others, mindful of James 3:1? What responsibility do I have for the spiritual values I pass on to others?

3. Do I take the Lord's Supper seriously? Before participating in the Lord's Supper, what specific preparations can I do in my life to make it more spiritually significant to me?

4. Have I fallen for the idea of "cheap grace," or do I respond gratefully to God's mercy by seeking to do His will? How do I see the balance between God's grace and my response in this matter of salvation?

5. How can I avoid the extremes of presumption and anxiety so that I can confidently walk with God every day? What distinguishes presumption from faith?

6. How might I be using religion for selfish motives, such as control over others? How can I let God use me? How can I be sure of my motives?

7. Do I understand the incarnational (that is, the union of the divine and the human) nature of revelation and inspiration? Can I accept cultural features of the Bible without losing confidence in its message? How can I distinguish between the message itself and the garments in which it was dressed?

■ Researching the Word

1. If you did not do so when you studied 2 Peter, use an exhaustive concordance to look up all the references in the Bible to Sodom and Gomorrah, and write a paragraph summarizing your findings.

2. Do the same for Balaam.

3. Study what is said about false teachers and false prophets elsewhere in the New Testament, beginning with the references you have seen in this chapter. Compare these descriptions and warnings with what Jude says. What similarities and differences do you observe? List these in your notebook. What reasons can you think of for these similarities and differences?

4. Using a concordance, find all the occurrences in the New Testament of the words *faith* and *grace*. Try to classify them according to their different meanings. Formulate a definition for each meaning.

■ Further Study of the Word

1. Perhaps you have already looked into 1 Enoch during your study of 2 Peter. For the *Assumption of Moses* (also called the *Testament of Moses*), see H. F. D. Sparks, *The Apocryphal Old Testament*, 601-616. Keep in mind that the ending of this work is missing.

2. In this chapter we have referred to a book called *The Wisdom of Solomon*, which is in the Apocrypha. The Old Testament Apocrypha are available in some editions of the King James Version as well as in many modern versions of the Scriptures. Probably the best version at present is found in those copies of the Revised Standard Version that contain the Apocrypha.

3. The question of which books properly belong in the Bible concerns the matter of the canon. For an extensive discussion of the canons of both the Old and New Testaments, see the articles in G. W. Bromiley, ed., *The International Standard Bible Encyclopedia*, 1:591-606. There is a somewhat briefer, but consequently less thorough, treatment in S. H. Horn, et. al., *Seventh-day Adventist Bible Dictionary*, 179-188. In addition, you may want to look at the article on "Pseudepigrapha" found on pages 913-915.

4. An adequate but conservative article on angels is in G. W. Bromiley, ed., *The International Standard Bible Encyclopedia*,

1:124-127. Its discussion of "the angel of the Lord" is balanced. See also the article on Michael in the S. H. Horn, et. al., *Seventh-day Adventist Bible Dictionary*, 736, 737. Note especially what this article has to say about the relation of the archangel Michael to the burial of Moses.

CHAPTER NINE

Challenges to Believers

Jude 20-25

In verse 3 Jude announced that his purpose was to urge his readers to "contend for the faith that was once for all entrusted to the saints." He then went into the reason why this was necessary. Only now, beginning in verse 20, does he return to positive instruction, thus fulfilling his announced purpose. In 20 to 23 Jude discusses aspects of how to contend for the faith. The English translation obscures the structure of this section, which consists of a series of parallel Greek imperatives, each with a dependent participle:

(20) "Build yourselves up in the most holy faith,
praying in the Holy Spirit.
(21) "Keep yourselves in the love of God,
waiting for the mercy of our Lord Jesus Christ unto eternal life.
(22) "Be merciful to the doubters, (23) save others,
snatching them from the fire.
"Be merciful to others in fear,
hating even the garment stained by the flesh" (personal translation).
(We have to recognize, however, that the text of verses 22, 23a has been corrupted, and the manuscripts exhibit many variations.)

The final two verses (vss. 24, 25) make a reassuring doxology.

■ Getting Into the Word

Jude 20-25

Read Jude from the beginning if you have forgotten what is in the earlier part. Then read Jude 20 to 25, and answer the following questions based on what you find in these verses.

1. How are verses 20 through 23 related to verse 3? How is the doxology of verses 24, 25 related to verses 4 through 19? How is it related to the greeting in verse 2?
2. What does Jude tell his readers to do for themselves?
3. What does Jude tell his readers to do for others?
4. To whom is the doxology of verses 24, 25 addressed? What does it tell us about the Trinity?
5. Notice that the word *keep* is used twice in this section (vss. 21, 24). Who does the keeping in each instance, and what is the relationship between the two?

■ Exploring the Word

How to Contend for the Faith

For the third time, Jude addresses his readers as "dear friends," contrasting the behavior that they need to exhibit with that of the false teachers described in verse 19. His instructions about how to "contend for the faith" consists of a series of imperatives (as expressed in English).

The first two imperatives are "*build yourselves up* in your most holy faith and *pray* in the Holy Spirit" (vs. 20, emphasis supplied). This is to be done both individually and collectively (the Greek verbs are in the plural). The New Testament calls for both kinds of upbuilding. First Thessalonians 5:11 says, "Encourage one another and build each other up." First Corinthians 14:12 says, "Try to excel in the gifts that build up the church." The church is a building; it is "God's household, built on the foundation of the apostles and prophets, with Christ Jesus himself as the chief cornerstone" (Eph. 2:19, 20). By building the church up on the biblical foundation, it can resist the divisive effects of the activities of the false teachers. This results in growth, though numerical growth is not what is in view here. Growth in the faith means deepening knowledge and commitment, increasing understanding of what Christ has done and of the response that Christ expects from us (compare 2 Pet. 3:18). Acts 2:42 tells us four ways by which the earliest church was nourished and built: devotion to the apostles' teaching (which for us is recorded in the New Testament), fellowship with each other for encouragement and support, the breaking of bread in table fellowship, especially in the Lord's Supper, and prayer.

"Pray," says Jude, "in the Holy Spirit" (vs. 20). Ephesians 6:18 also tells us to pray in the Spirit, and Romans 8:26 explains the reason for it (compare Gal. 4:6). Christian prayer is *to* the Father, *through* the Son, and *in* the Holy Spirit. Christian prayer is *inspired* prayer. The best prayer is when God talks to Himself through us.

It is doubtful whether the false teachers prayed at all. If they did, they did it only in public for show. And instead of building up the church, they divided it. They needed to hear Paul's warning to the Corinthians about damaging the church: "Don't you know that you yourselves are God's temple and that God's Spirit lives in you? If anyone destroys God's temple [the church], God will destroy him; for God's temple is sacred, and you are that temple" (1 Cor. 3:16, 17).

The next imperative is "keep yourselves in God's love" (vs. 21). The Greek could mean either our love for God or God's love for us, but the latter meaning is a little more likely because it comports with other similar sayings. Paul prays that the Ephesians may be "rooted and established in love" (Eph. 3:17). Jesus said, "Remain in my love" (John 15:9), and it is important to notice that this is done by obeying Christ's commands (vs. 10). This was something the false teachers were not interested in.

Thus we have a part to play in maintaining our vital connection with God. This is the way to await Christ's second coming. That is the meaning of "as you wait for the mercy of our Lord Jesus Christ" (vs. 21). When Christ shall come, He will bring judgment for the ungodly and mercy for the godly (2 Tim. 1:18), which will issue in eternal life. That is when the merciful will obtain mercy (Matt. 5:7).

So the next imperative is "be merciful to those who doubt" (vs. 22). We should note that many manuscripts say "convince those who doubt." Whichever variant is correct, here, Jude begins to tell his readers what they must do for others, having gotten their own spiritual house in order. "Snatch others from the fire and save them" (vs. 23) is reminiscent of Zechariah 3:2, "Is not this man a burning stick snatched from the fire?" It is a verse Jude had previously alluded to in verse 9.

It was possible to rescue not only those who had been deceived by the false teachers, but the false teachers themselves, though that project should be undertaken with great caution: "To others show mercy, mixed with fear—hating even the clothing stained by corrupted flesh" (vs. 23). This may be an allusion to Zechariah 3:4. The Greek word for clothing here is *chitōn*, which is the garment worn next to the skin. In the process of curing the sick, the healer must take care that he himself not be infected, and the same is true of spiritual healers. Yet the risk must be taken as Jesus took the risk: "It is not the healthy who need a doctor, but the sick. I have not come to call the righteous, but sinners" (Mark 2:17).

Doxology

Doxology is ascription of praise, glorifying God, and that is what we have in the last two verses of Jude (vss. 24, 25). Many New Testament epistles end with a benediction, and some contain doxologies, but the only other epistles that end with a doxology are Romans (a long one, Romans 16:25-27) and 2 Peter (a short one).

But to whom, precisely, is the doxology lifted up, to God the Father or to Jesus Christ? The formula reads, "To the only God our Savior be glory . . . through Jesus Christ our Lord" (vs. 25). The preposition *through* clearly marks a distinction between the two members of the Godhead, and it is God the Father who is called Saviour here. In the New Testament, Christ is more often called the Saviour, but there are eight times the title is applied to the Father (besides here, the places are Luke 1:47; 1 Timothy 1:1; 2:3; 4:10; Titus 1:3; 2:10; 3:4). Interestingly, in two adjacent verses, Titus 1:3 and 1:4, first God and then Christ Jesus are called "our Savior." It is all part of the mystery of the Trinity, three yet one, sharing attributes and titles. The resultant language is often paradoxical. Here, God, distinguished from Christ, is called "the only God," which sounds like a rigid monotheism that has no room for the deity of Christ. (The same usage is found in John 5:44; 17:3; Revelation 15:4.) But here, also, Jesus Christ is called "our Lord," a divine title found throughout the Old Testament and the New. The mystery must remain that, for only God can fully comprehend God.

God, says Jude 24, "*is able* to keep you from falling" (emphasis added). Two other New Testament doxologies begin similarly. God "*is able* to establish you by my gospel," says Paul (Rom. 16:25, emphasis added). He "*is able* to do immeasurably more than all we ask or imagine" (Eph. 3:20, emphasis added). If God is able to keep us from falling, why do some fall, as was shown in verse 5? Verse 24 must be linked with verse 21, which points out the human role. We meet here another mystery. Throughout the history of theology, some have insisted on divine sovereignty, and others, upon human responsibility. Is salvation only God's work, or must we play a part? This classic debate with many ramifications began with Augustine and Pelagius in the fifth century, continued in the seventeenth century between the Calvinist scholastics and Arminius, and is not settled yet. The fact is, both sides are completely right! We can do no better than to cling to the paradox of Philippians 2:12, 13.

God is able not only to keep you from falling; He is able to "present you before his glorious presence without fault with great joy" (vs. 24). It is mind-boggling to think that God can make us fit to come into the very place of His Shekinah glory, which stands for God Himself. Sacrificial victims offered in the temple had to be without fault, unblemished (Lev. 1:3; 3:1). Paul also said that God can make us like that (Col. 1:22; Eph. 1:4; 5:27; 1 Thess. 5:23). He does this by making Christ's sinless life and sacrificial death count as ours, for Christ was without fault. The fulfillment of this supreme experience, when we shall be ushered into the presence of the divine glory itself, is eschatological. It will happen at the great Day, if we do not fall.

It is through Jesus Christ that our praises—to God be "glory, majesty, power and authority"—are passed on to the Father (vs. 25). The God-man is our link and channel. The doxology continues to explode in mind-boggling words that echo through the heavens: "before all ages, now and forevermore! Amen" (vs. 24).

Thus our study of Jude comes to an end in praise—and in mystery.

■ Applying the Word

Jude 20-25

1. What am I doing to build up myself and my brothers and sisters in the faith—in our understanding and commitment to the message of Christ and about Christ?
2. Do I pray in the Holy Spirit? Do I know what it means to pray in the Spirit? Have I prayed that the Holy Spirit will help me to pray in the Holy Spirit?
3. What specific things can I incorporate into my devotional life to keep myself in God's love, trusting Him to save me?
4. What am I doing to snatch sinners and doubters from the fire? How much risk am I willing to take? How much is too much risk?
5. How do I react and feel when I come into the presence of the unfathomable things of God and their mystery? Why?
6. Do I really know how to praise and glorify God? List nonverbal ways to praise God. How many are a part of my life?

■ Researching the Word

1. With the help of a concordance, look up all the occurrences of the word *Saviour*, and try to determine who is meant. Divide a page in your Jude notebook into columns,

and list the texts under such headings as "Christ," "the Father," etc.

2. Using both a concordance and the marginal notes in your Bible, try to find out all you can about the role of the Holy Spirit in prayer and worship. Write a paragraph or two summarizing what you discover.

3. Depending on your Bible translation, look up the words *fault* or *blemish* or *defect*. Describe the Old Testament background of these terms. Then study how they are used in the New Testament.

■ Further Study of the Word

1. The doctrine of the Trinity and the issue of divine sovereignty versus human responsibility and free will are key issues with many implications in theological debate. You may want to study the issues in a book about the history of theology or systematic theology. On the Trinity, see the booklet by G. Wheeler, *Is God a Committee?* A conservative Calvinist approach to the issues is provided by L. Berkhof, *Systematic Theology*. There are also appropriate articles in the many dictionaries of systematic theology, historical theology, and Biblical theology.

2. On the expression "the only God," see E. Stauffer, *New Testament Theology*, 242-244.

.